SOMETHING SOMEBODY STOLE

A PERSONAL JOURNEY TO SOUL RECOVERY AFTER 20 YEARS IN A CONTROVERSIAL RELIGIOUS CULT

Ray Connolly

Copyright © 2011 Ray Connolly
All rights reserved.

ISBN: 1460922549
ISBN-13: 9781460922545
LCCN: 2011902607
CreateSpace, Charleston, South Carolina

*Dedicated to
Aimee and Rebecca
and their family and friends*

TABLE OF CONTENTS

Dedication / iii
Contents / v
Acknowledgements / vii
Introduction / ix
Epigraph / xii
Chapter One: Hitchhiking Back to Eden / 1
Chapter Two: Life Before Mapquest / 9
Chapter Three: Down the Rabbit Hole / 21
Chapter Four: Numbers and Exodus / 31
Chapter Five: The Plot Thickens / 41
Chapter Six: Hotel California / 49
Chapter Seven: Cracks in the Dyke / 57
Chapter Eight: The Fork in the Road / 69
Chapter Nine: Zombies and Serpents / 81
Chapter Ten: O Brother, Who Art Thou? / 93
Chapter Eleven: The Fellowship of the Wrong / 103
Chapter Twelve: Heart of Darkness / 113
Chapter Thirteen: Speaking of the Unspeakable / 125
Chapter Fourteen: Your God Is Too Weird / 137
Chapter Fifteen: How Firm a Foundation? / 149
Chapter Sixteen: Another Look at the Book / 161
Chapter Seventeen: This Is Your Brain on Pain / 169
Chapter Eighteen: The F Word / 181
Chapter Nineteen: And Now Back to Our Story / 191
Chapter Twenty: Long and Winding Road / 203
Endnotes / 215

ACKNOWLEDGEMENTS

There are many folks that deserve acknowledgement, although I'm not sure if they all would appreciate the connection.

First of all, thank you to Bob and Judy Pardon of Meadowhaven for their help to us personally, and in our grasp of issues of thought reform, spiritual abuse, and recovery.

Thanks to the many fellow travelers who read my various drafts and helped clarify the focus of the text, especially Phil, George, Hap, Debbie, Ginny, Sam, Ralph, Joanne, Jeanne, Claudia, Kit, Bernadette and most especially Carol, who went way above and beyond and was merciless with my style, grammar, thinking and evasions. Ouch!

Thanks to Brian McLaren, for his words of encouragement. They were such a timely gift.

Thanks to those who helped type early drafts: Anna, Aladdin, and Stephanie. Thanks to Christian for technical and design assistance.

Thanks to my family, for not throwing me out...especially Stephanie! I love you!

And...thanks be to God. (Although He may wish to disavow any connection to the project.)

INTRODUCTION

As I was writing this book I sent out an early draft to a number of friends who were kind enough to share their feedback to help me sharpen its focus. The most common question I heard back was: "Who are you writing this book for?" Frankly, it's not an easy question to answer.

I think perhaps first of all I wrote it for myself. It has been quite a therapeutic exercise. I have attempted not only to capture the bare bones of my experience of over twenty years in a highly controversial religious group, but also to reflect upon the lengthy and painful process of trying to recover from its impact.

Secondly, I wrote in the hope that sharing my personal journey and some of the discoveries I have made along the way—often through the insights (and words) of others—might be helpful to those traveling a similar road. If you are in this category, I hope my struggles may shed a little light on the path as you pick your way through the pieces of your personal apocalypse.

Thirdly, I had in mind the many people who have had a close encounter with a group like this through a relative or loved one who gets involved in a cult. The mysterious psychological dynamics of a "true believer" can be frustratingly perplexing to the one on outside looking in. It is my hope that this account may offer some clues as to the nature of the experience to those seeking to understand.

Finally, I must confess that I write in the hopes that my kids will at least have some record of my thought process when they ponder the issue of "what the heck were they thinking?" An explanation is not a justification. But at least it's an explanation.

SOMETHING SOMEBODY STOLE

The story is, of course, based on my personal experience. I tried to include enough personal detail to put the issues explored into some sort of comprehensible context. For a long time people who heard parts of my story would tell me, "You should write a book." My response was that I couldn't figure out whether it would be a testimony, an exposé, or a confession. In the end I guess it's a little of each. But I am not trying to tell my whole life's story here. I like what Lily Tomlin said in reference to her teenage diary: "What if it's boring...or if it's not boring, it might be too revealing. Or worse, it might be too revealing and still be boring." With this idea in mind, I went with a more analytical and often more general explanation of the issues, with just enough personal stuff that it might make a little more sense to the uninitiated.

Let me make one last note before getting started. "The Family" (the specific group I was involved with) is a highly controversial group on the fringe even among fringe groups. There was, of course, and continues to be an evolution—or perhaps better described as a devolution—throughout its history. The group I joined is not the group I left. And the group I left is not even the group that continues to exist around the world today. Beliefs and practices have changed over time and differ from place to place, making each person's experience quite unique. (In fact, as I'm finalizing this manuscript, the Family is going through a fairly dramatic revamping of its practices and policies, which hopefully may eliminate a repetition of many of the abuses of the past.) My characterization of the group reflects my own experience of it. For others, I am certain, it was very different.

The particular issue that most often surfaces whenever the group the Family is discussed today is the devastating effects of its highly unusual sexual beliefs and practices, including the founder's disastrous (and criminal!) exploration of adult/child sexual contact. The subject has hurt so many young lives that it has come to dominate any examination of the group's impact. But it is a subject that emerged only over time and was not central to most of my overall personal experience. With this in mind, I have tried to discuss it in a somewhat

INTRODUCTION

compartmentalized way. I take this approach in the hope that the look into the cult experience could remain somewhat universal, and not swallowed up in this one particular aberration somewhat unique to the Family, as weighty as the subject may be.

I do talk about the issue in several places in the narrative, and have devoted a separate chapter to the subject at one point in story. I hope that any ex-Family second generation readers will understand that it is not my intention to in any way minimize the issue. It is, in fact, central to the understanding of the extent of the dangers involved in the social psychology of cults. I hope that by presenting it in the context of at least one first generation member's overall experience, that perhaps this perspective may add to the understanding of this darkest of all the dark products that cult life can engender.

Anyway, with that said, I'm going to try to begin back at the beginning.

In the middle of the night
I go walking in my sleep
Through the valley of fear
To the river so deep

I've been searching for something
Taken out of my soul
Something I'd never lose
Something somebody stole

~Billy Joel, "River of Dreams"

CHAPTER 1

HITCHHIKING BACK TO EDEN

*I came upon a child of God
He was walking along the road
And I asked him where are you goin'
And he told me...
We are stardust
We are golden
And we've got to get ourselves
Back to the garden.*

~ Joni Mitchell, "Woodstock"

Why did God make you?

~ Lesson 1, Question 6, from the *Baltimore Catechism*

Spring 1970. My brief academic career at the College of the Holy Cross was starting to fray badly at the intersection of man's endless search for meaning and the clarity that one experiences in a cloud of marijuana smoke. The "system" was losing its grip on me as I sat cross-legged, watching closely for the dawning of the Age Of

Aquarius. The moon may have been in the seventh house, and Jupiter aligned with Mars, but all was not well in my Woodstock world. I was becoming increasingly aware, through an amplifier of psychoactive substances combined with many hours of serious self-absorption, that "the system" was not my only problem. Peace and love guiding the planets sounded good enough. But I realized that I had no power to love...and that knowledge left me little peace. Somewhere down in my "inner child," the Baltimore Catechism and the good Sisters of Charity were busily gnawing at my insides. I was one unhappy hippy.

Depending on how many "born again" conversion testimonies you've heard from that era, you might be beginning to see all the classic elements of plot starting to come together. The gap between the happiness I envisioned and the rotten feeling in the pit of my stomach was growing ever larger. I liked movies with dark themes and sad endings, meaningful conversations with friends about the meaninglessness of it all, listening to the blues and smoking cigarettes on rainy days. I was really starting to warm up to the role. I can remember imagining how thoughtful I must have looked while brooding, and then catching myself and feeling so embarrassed about being so vain...like some hippy version of John Travolta checking himself out in the mirror before going to the disco. Sheesh. I was depressed and getting more depressed about being depressed. It all sounds pretty clichéd now, but at the time life felt like some sort of inescapable madness...a guy looking in a mirror seeing himself looking in a mirror while looking in a mirror, etc.

I had been raised Catholic, so of course I'd heard a lot about Jesus. While I was growing up it seemed to me that Jesus was huge, like that gigantic statue of Him on the mountain overlooking the harbor of Rio de Janeiro. Yet at the same time His personality was pretty blurred. He jumped from being a baby in the manger to a rosy-cheeked shepherd in a snowy robe, eyes cast hazily at half-mast. Then He'd morph into the difficult-to-think-about torture victim hanging (for reasons never fully explained) on the crucifix. Then He'd transform again into the ever-present, all-seeing eye staring into the hidden recesses of my soul. He seemed to be scrutinizing, with a mixture of sorrow and anger, the nasty mess that lived inside me—the stuff that I would much prefer remain unobserved. I did sincerely believe the whole deal, trying sporadically to stay in "the state of grace" for as high a percentage of the time as possible; or, failing that, trying to avoid getting hit by a car before I could make it to back to confession.

I have some memories, perhaps retouched over the years in the light of subsequent insights, but which I can still recall with almost palpable emotion. There were times kneeling by my bedside in my pajamas, earnestly pleading for forgiveness for some petty crime or seven-year-old sin of omission or commission, searching my little heart for a sense of divine forgiveness. I would often fall asleep counting "ejaculations." (For you non-Catholics, this is the term for brief, one-line prayers such as "Jesus, Mary, and Joseph, pray for us." Thankfully, the term seems to have fallen by the wayside…as it now becomes in its ambiguity almost an occasion of sin in itself.) These brief prayers would be offered up as "spiritual bouquets" to shorten the suffering of the souls doing hard time in purgatory. That seems like a lot of pressure to put on a seven-year-old. There were also many moments of excruciating boredom, to the point of near loss of consciousness, while saying decades of the Rosary in Mary's month of May with the whole student body of Our Lady of Sorrows Elementary. On such occasions the parish seemed particularly aptly named. We gathered in the noonday heat by Our Lady's flower-strewn grotto, which was particularly challenging after a carb-heavy cafeteria lunch and a competitive game of dodge ball in the parking lot. At such times one could begin to imagine how those children in Fatima started seeing visions and hearing voices.

My favorite liturgy was the Stations of the Cross. During Lent we would gather in the almost transcendental atmosphere of the Gothic architecture of the church. The quality of light was ethereal, filtered by stained glass and dimly reflected off the massive granite block walls. After some quiet meditation, tripping out a little on the rows of flickering votive candles in the translucent red glass containers, our attention drifted towards the small procession of altar boys with various holy paraphernalia. My favorite was that ornate golden censor swinging back and forth on a chain, clicking with each motion, distributing swirling smoke signals heavy with frankincense. Is it any wonder I was predisposed to experimenting with psychedelics? The priest followed in his amazingly eye-catching vestments, looking like a medieval Elton John. The group would make its way to fourteen stations commemorating the various sufferings of Jesus during His passion and crucifixion. At each stop a brief meditation would be read followed by a quatrain, chanted to a Gregorian beat by the congregation. The words were designed to bring home to each of us in a deeply personal way that each act of selfless sacrifice was done specifically for us. I spilled more than a few salty tears on my clip-on tie and may have soiled the cuffs of my white school shirt with the emotions that seemed to trigger an involuntary response from my nose. I can't help but think that God may have jotted a quick "note to self" that would single me out for closer personal attention further down the line.

Upon entering my teen years, the struggle to try and stay in the state of grace became way too much of a hassle. I was quickly developing a new set of priorities. I recognized that in all probability, hell, or if I was really lucky, at the very least some very serious time in purgatory, would be my destiny. This was not a train of thought inviting lengthy periods of contemplation at the time though...what a buzz kill.

Eventually, during my adolescent struggles to emerge from the chrysalis of childhood, I began to turn away from the certainty of God being real. All the typical arguments occurred to me with such a texture of originality that at the time I thought that I was the first one who had ever thought of them. This also gave me a convenient line of discussion with my conscience whenever that ol' Jiminy Cricket began to chirp a little too loudly. This was followed by the usual sparkling insights of youth into the hypocrisy of the religious establishment—another one of the "Top Ten Reasons Not to Let the God Thing Get in Your Way." To that was added a few dashes of barely understood Sartre and Camus, along with the growing pressure of teenage hormones, and Jesus began to fade in my consciousness to little more than a faint smudge mark left by a poorly maintained eraser.

After taking a brief dip in the pool of leftist radical chic that was in vogue at the time (who could resist a good deal on a Mao jacket or a poster of Che?), my continuing search for meaning led me into that mist of strawberry scented, New Age vagueness. Some of it had a little spiritual tingle to it, if you did not try to focus too carefully on it for too long, which could give you a slight headache. But as far as providing any real footing…well…it was more like trying to walk across a waterbed while slightly inebriated.

Every once in a while a picture, a line from a song, a phrase in a book, or some inexplicable roadside graffiti would catch my attention, and that strange Nazarene would momentarily pop back across my mind. But I'd think of Him as some sort of historical hippie figure, some avatar perhaps, with a slightly Abbie Hoffman vibe to Him. Nothing along the lines of a "savior" or anything like that. But still, these glimpses felt like refreshing breezes that would briefly cool the desert in my soul. Something unidentifiable seemed to be gently tugging at my heart, drawing me back towards this fascinating figure. But it seemed like such a gauche solution to the problem. Surely it must be something more esoteric, something less dangerous to the ego, something well, groovier.

During my sophomore year in college things started coming to a head. The depression that seemed to hover about me like Pigpen's ever-present dust cloud was growing more visible and oppressive. My relationship with others became difficult. I built a tent in my dorm room out of Indian print bedspread to avoid contact with others. I can remember feeling as though we were all separated from each other by these invisible Pepsodent shields. But what was more disturbing was the unraveling of my relationship with my girlfriend of three-plus years.

Ginny and I had begun dating in our junior year of high school. We each went to our respective Catholic boy's and girl's schools in the same New Jersey town. A deeply emotional bond developed between us. We'd shared each other's rites of passage through our silly and serious mid-teens on into our college years. She had been a thoughtful, somewhat shy, folk-music-loving, volunteer-working and sincerely religious girl. I had been a thoughtful, somewhat rowdy, drinking, brawling, but still poetry-reading irreligious guy with a penchant for petty crime. I'm not sure how we clicked, but the connection grew deep and strong and clearly way past puppy love. I can't really say exactly how it affected her, but I can say her love and friendship had helped steer me away from some pretty scary precipices. Our relationship had become my very center of gravity.

But now it was wobbling badly, and our bond was tearing in places. Our relationship became a frustrating cycle of disturbing, almost compulsive selfishness on my part followed by tearful letters of shamed apologies to her a few days later. In one such Monday missive I quoted a few lines from Biff Rose, an offbeat songwriter of the time:

Your fairness and easiness is all I ever see,
So I'm going downtown where it's always loud,
gonna lose myself in the downtown crowd,
So I can find...what's gnawing at me.[1]

My inability to love someone so loving and lovable was just so painful to observe in action. I was really starting to get on my own nerves. Psychedelics began seeping into the picture. If one is disturbingly dissatisfied with one's interior landscape, this is a remarkably bad idea.

All things seemed to converge as I was sitting on the gym floor of a little YMCA at a remarkable solo concert in-the-round by an as yet little known singer-songwriter, James Taylor. He was seated at half court on a folding chair, fresh from several visits to rehabilitation and psychiatric institutions. As he tuned his guitar, there was something about the look in his eye that told you that he still wasn't entirely sure whether to go all in on the widely accepted definition of reality. The overall effect was enough to make me rethink some of my own bets, too.

The next day I withdrew from school. Draft or no draft, I was off to walk the country road.

CHAPTER 2

LIFE BEFORE MAPQUEST

*I shall be telling this with a sigh
Somewhere ages and ages hence:
Two roads diverged in a wood, and I
I took the one less traveled by,
And that has made all the difference.*

~ Robert Frost, "The Road Not Taken"

*Sometimes the road less traveled
is less traveled for a reason.*

~ Jerry Seinfeld

I followed my thumb for the next few months up and down the East Coast, visiting friends and strangers. Through the kaleidoscopic lens of the times and various herbal sacraments, like some comic strip Sherlock following footprints with a magnifying glass I earnestly searched for clues. This led to a series of unpleasant self-revelations of my own murky inner motivations. As my sense of alienation grew and I became more attuned to the gyrations of the needle of my internal compass, a weird string of events unfolded in which the God factor seemed to leave an eerie echo.

I remember the last date I had with my gentle and upbeat girlfriend. We shared some mescaline and headed to a movie theater where we had hoped to see a Beatles film, but instead found the Rolling Stones film *Sympathy for the Devil* playing. This I took as a very bad omen. After deciding to pass on that movie, we walked through a park where an elderly Catholic gentleman handed me a prayer card. In what I immediately recognized as a cosmic coincidence, the card was the same color as the tab of mescaline we'd taken. The card bore a message informing me that "God, to whom you belong" was seeking me. After a few glances over my shoulder to check, we finally ended up making our way to a film somewhat prophetically titled *The End of the Road*. It was a weird and depressing exploration of madness. It left me feeling like I was being yanked away from this bright, good girl whom I had been infecting with my dark nature, and was being pulled out into some place God could get His hands on me without disturbing the rest of the class. Truth be told, in a way I think that was what was happening.

This was followed by another strange journey where I got unintentionally, and seemingly unavoidably, emotionally intimate with a good friend's fiancée. I guiltily fled away by thumb once again, only to get waylaid for hours at an interstate entrance ramp with almost no traffic. It was my habit to try and carry some small paperback to read in such circumstances. Before leaving my friend's house I had scanned his bookshelf and found I had pretty much read all that was there, except a pocket-size Catholic Daily Missal that caught my curiosity, and which he extended to me with his blessing. While awaiting friendly conveyance southward, I began to browse through the red lettered readings from the Gospels. I was suddenly gripped by a passage from the seventeenth chapter of John. Jesus was speaking to God in a manner that sent shivers up my spine. When he spoke to "Father," he clearly knew to whom he was speaking. Really well. This was no vague meditation on the connectedness of all energy, but something really specific and personal, yet at the same time amazingly transcendent. And it really set me to wondering again...

Already feeling a bit shaky from these episodes, there followed another self-shattering experience with an oddly mismatched encounter group in which my inability to love unselfishly was pinpointed with surprising accuracy by a fourteen-year-old, semi-literate juvenile delinquent: "You talk about loving everyone, but you don't even know how to love me!" This left me sobbing uncontrollably, much to the embarrassment and mild panic of the facilitator, who in an effort to calm me down suggested maybe the Wednesday night group might work better for me. This insight did not quite nail it for me.

This incident was immediately followed by the sudden arrival of my younger brother back from a trip to California. Paul had an odd glow about him, like Bilbo Baggins returning to the Shire after his adventures with the dwarves and such. When he arrived home, I happened to be up in my room sharing a little "pipeweed" with some friends. Paul's California adventure tales of working in a circus with refugees from the Hell's Angels and his struggles to save mankind by throwing rocks at cops at People's Park suddenly took a turn into some even stranger terrain.

He started to recount the story of a former acidhead named Chris who had experienced a religious conversion after an encounter with a street preacher. Chris in turn began attempting to evangelize my brother, who had been crashing in the same house. Paul's Marxist outlook initially enabled him to fend off such attempts with the usual "opiate of the people" rejoinders. That is, up until the final night of his West Coast sojourn, when he decided to drop some acid in hopes of achieving a summing up reflection upon his California experience. His trip slid rapidly into a genuine bummer in which a growing physical weight pressed down on him as glimpses of his self-deceptions flashed through his conscience. His converted housemate Chris offered some biblical insights as to what was going on in Paul's soul, which led eventually to a particularly urgent Sinner's Prayer.

The strange glow on my brother's face as he told the story seemed to indicate that Jesus had indeed responded to the invitation.

This new information definitely had a somewhat cooling effect on our friendly little smoke-in. Our buddies suddenly all remembered places they were supposed to be, and headed out with some unexplained haste.

But the impact on me it was completely different. My heartbeat began to quicken like the clicking of a Geiger counter honing in on radium. Something new and important was drawing me forward in the quest. I wanted to know how to have this experience. I felt like Charlton Heston as he caught a glimpse of the burning bush: "I will turn aside and see this strange sight." Unfortunately my brother had "gotten saved" just an hour or so before he had to leave for New Jersey, and knew little more than that one "must accept Christ" and that it was all explained in the pocket New Testament he'd been given to by his friend before departing from Berkeley. So we spent much of the next several days trying to find the "How to Accept Christ" passage in the Bible. Although we found some pretty cool stuff—like the amazing "lilies of the field...birds of the air" thing, which had quite a lot of appeal—those step-by-step instructions on acquiring eternal life proved somewhat elusive.

During these few days I grew so focused on the God question that I actually woke up one night with the words *Is God really there? Is God really there?* ringing over and over in my mind. Finally, I decided that perhaps I should simply ask and find out. So I screwed up my courage and spoke out into the dark with nervous sincerity, "God, if you are really there, speak to me." I grew quiet, expectant, fighting the urge to rebuke myself for going right over the edge. I felt like a deer happened upon in the woods that seems to freeze, standing perfectly still except for the slight twitching of its ears as it seeks some confirmation of the presence it had sensed on the edge of its consciousness.

As was my habit, I'd left a small radio playing softly in the corner of the room as a hedge against the silence in case I awoke in the night depressed. But suddenly a line from a song that was playing seemed to leap out, framed, hanging in the air like a neon sign in the dark room. I can't recall who was singing, but the lyric was unforgettable: "You don't talk to no one who don't talk to you." As I let this sink in, a feeling began to grow inside of me. The thought bubbled up: *I haven't talked to God in years. Is that why I haven't heard Him talking to me? Now, here, the first time I let myself become childlike enough to break the silence, it seems like I get this answer.* Yeah, it was just the radio, but it could have been playing "Paint It Black" or "Get Off of My Cloud" or "They're Coming to Take Me Away." It was not quite John Wesley's "strange warming of the heart" conversion at Aldersgate, or Augustine's "take and read" epiphany in ancient Italy. Still, for me it really felt like God was there. And He wanted to talk.

After a few more days of unsuccessfully searching the New Testament for easy to follow directions on the side of the box, I decided to set off for California to track down my brother's friend Chris, who had apparently discovered the secret of the universe, in hopes the he might hook me up. Equipped with my well-worn Boy Scouts of America backpack and a fairly experienced thumb, I got dropped at an entrance to the New Jersey Turnpike by my brother. His parting words were something like, "I get this feeling you're gonna find what you've been looking for." And then some, as it turned out!

I remember the trip as taking on something of a mythic quality in my mind. It was May of 1970, and the Beatles' "Let It Be" seemed to be playing everywhere, reinforcing my sense of guidance. "There will be an answer" became sort of my internal mantra. I remember getting stuck in the middle of the night somewhere in Ohio, and actually having the police give me a lift, hippie though I was, to a better spot to hitchhike. At the time, this felt like a genuine, God-really-does-love-me miracle.

In Chicago I visited a thoughtful friend from high school, who was now into Baha'i. She gave me some literature to read, which was anything but the "simplicity of Christ" that I was seeking. I remember getting a little depressed by this stuff, and went out to wander and ponder through the streets of Chicago. I was drawn into a church that had an open Bible lying on the pew. The passage, which I cannot recall, somehow spoke to me about getting back on the search, and I was once again sticking out my thumb, pilgrim's determination renewed.

I remember having to pretty much walk through St. Louis (not too many hippies around there yet) before finally getting picked up by a Volkswagen bug with a "Smile, God loves you!" smiley face bumper sticker and "Let It Be" playing on the radio. I remember thanking God...a strangely exhilarating act of faith.

My next ride was from an army deserter headed for Santa Barbara, California. He was kind of quiet company for the next few days, but since I had a friend living in Santa Barbara (the only person I actually knew who lived west of Chicago) I again felt the hand of Providence upon me. We finally arrived at my friend Billy's stylish beachfront apartment to a welcome of California wine and Mexican marijuana. He had an incredible view of the Pacific Ocean, an expansive record collection, and serious stereo setup. When I began to note that the local population seemed to be heavily weighted in favor of bikini clad young ladies that were a New Jersey boy's California fantasy, my inner compass needle was temporarily sent spinning in all directions. What was it I was looking for again?

But the next morning I awoke to that same haunting emptiness and yearning. I felt pulled like a tide in the full moon. I walked out on the beach with waves rolling up to my feet and tears rolling down my cheeks. I desperately prayed: "God, I am really messing up. I don't know how to love. I hurt even those I really care about and can't seem to stop myself. I want You to take over. If You will show me the truth in life, I promise You, Lord, I will do it." I know, dangerous words, but as I have joked with some of my fellow travelers, it seemed like a good idea at the time.

I dropped my girlfriend another postcard: *Beginning to wrestle with the "concept of a personal God." Got to stop and get back to loving Jesus. God protect me, please.*

Back at the apartment after a few brief words over coffee, I arranged to meet my host Billy at the football stadium, where that day Jerry Rubin of Chicago Seven fame was addressing the student populace on some absurdly naïve, plant-induced plan to levitate the Pentagon, or the like. That afternoon, unable to find Billy in the forty thousand or so hippies, yippies, and weekend trippies who were gathered, I drifted in my usual alienated way to the back row of the stadium to observe. Some conga playing and chanting provided a backdrop for water balloon fights. Sunny Santa Barbara just didn't seem to be the right setting for Lenin and Trotsky to resurface, I'm afraid. What I later came to realize was a "Jesus Freak" jumped up on the stage and started trying to preach Jesus amid heckling and water balloons. People seated near me snickered condescendingly, and although a part of me felt like snickering, too, another part of me felt extremely uncomfortable with this reaction. Maybe that guy, as embarrassingly uncool as he was, knew something the rest of us didn't?

Finally Jerry arrived to an almost rock star reception, and he began to "Yeah, man!" his message with clenched fist salutes punctuating his thoughts. The logic of his exhortation seemed to wander a bit, though I doubt too many in the crowd noticed, given the aroma wafting through the stands.

Suddenly, something really different started happening. Into the stadium, a long line of maybe fifty or so young men and women, longhaired but decidedly not traveling with the same circus, flowed slowly and deliberately into the stadium. They were clothed in red burlap robes, carrying seven-foot long staves and Scripture-inscribed scrolls. Their foreheads were smudged with ashes, and their eyes were staring eerily off to some point in space slightly above their normal line of sight, as though they were peering through a tear in the dimension. Several of them were carrying a makeshift coffin, draped in an American flag with an air of solemnity that clearly indicated they were acting out a mock funeral for the nation. Some of the yippies started to approach as though they might begin to target these mourners with water bombs, but Jerry told them to back off.

He seemed to respect the gravity of their demeanor, even though it put a slight damper on the revolution-by-party atmosphere of the occasion. Slowly they wound their way up the stadium stairs and circled around, drawing to a halt to with a resounding crash of the rods, just feet away from where I sat.

The intense, almost frightening, otherworldly expressions on their faces, coupled with the apocalyptic Scriptures lamenting judgments soon to fall, somehow made the day's scheduled goings on seem a tad silly. Part of me was thinking, *Oh boy, everything I ever heard about Southern California is true. I wonder when Charles Manson arrives?* But another part of me was in some way saying, "Amen," though as yet I still had no idea what I was amening. The sheer weight of the atmosphere they carried, disturbing though it was, somehow resonated with the sense of profundity I had attached to my own personal odyssey. Still, I can't say it was an instant "yes!" within me. More of a "hmmm...I wonder..."

As the speeches and spectacles drew to a close, these peculiar prophets filtered out as solemnly as they had entered through the gates and out of view. I drifted out with the crowd, feeling more separated than ever and disquieted by what I had witnessed. The biblical expression "We have seen strange things today" sort of sums up my state of mind. Somewhat dazed, I found myself approaching a spot where the red-robed ones had regrouped. Having shed their sackcloth for more conventional jeans and T-shirts, they were now gathered in small pockets and singing with guitars or handing out sandwiches, and beginning to engage in personalized preaching. They challenged the weekend revolutionaries with a compelling conviction. I was slowly drawn into the scene. I watched as a young student with "church member" practically embroidered on his shirt tried to defend his position as a member of "the system" while still serving Jesus. The prophet, now in civilian garb, slowly flipped his large Bible to a red-lettered passage, inviting the student to read it out loud..."No man can serve two masters," then, "Whosoever forsaketh not all that he hath," and then "All that believed were together and had all things common." Each quote was met with a slightly more defensive "But..." as the student grew more flustered. I was frankly somewhat amazed by the exchange on several levels: by the radical content of the quotations, which were completely unfamiliar to me, as well as by the surprising fact that anyone even knew what was in the Bible, much less where it was found, and that they actually seemed to want to base their very life on its implications!

Eventually one of the more recently converted must have picked up on my fascination and asked me if I had yet "met Jesus." I stumbled and stuttered, "Well, not yet, I don't think, but I'm starting to get close, I think...I'm not sure what you mean..." I met his next advance with some defense mechanism from left field, asking him what he believed about life on other planets. This seemed to throw him a little, as I later learned he'd only "known the Lord" for a week himself. But the dodge only delayed the inevitable, as he then called over his more experienced colleague. This one quickly cut through the fog with some surprisingly piercing eyes that seemed to be cataloging my inner secrets. He point blank asked me whether I wanted "to know Jesus or not?"

Fear swirled through me in a flash. What if I tried it and it turned out not to work? What would be left then? Or, what if Jesus did show up and He turned out to be a real dork? What if these people would then have me, and I would be forced to follow them, with my arms outstretched in front of me and my pupils spinning as I was marched back to their camp to meet their pied piper? Wouldn't now be a good time for a cigarette break? But finally something just told that voice inside my head to shush, and I was on my knees in the middle of that field, eyes squeezed shut and holding hands with this complete stranger, repeating the Sinner's Prayer. After uttering those now familiar phrases I went off on some improvisational prayer riff of my own, tears streaming down my cheeks, struggling to catch my breath, and eventually closing with an "amen" before having to wipe my rapidly running nose with my sleeve.

SOMETHING SOMEBODY STOLE

When I opened my eyes again, it seemed to me that someone had taken the polyethylene wrapper off the world. The clouds moved slowly with some silent music. A quiet settled on my soul. I smiled as the brothers rejoiced with those unfamiliar "Praise the Lord, hallelujahs!" that no longer sounded so strange to my ears. I think a little tentative "hallelujah" may have even escaped my own lips. "So *that's* how you accept Christ," I thought to myself, more than a little pleased. Something that I later found out was called "joy" began to rise within my being. I felt really, really clean.

We sat as the team shared some verses with me over a peanut butter and banana sandwich as guitar music played in the background. Zealous conversations were accompanied by a lot more eye contact then I was used to. The occasional "hallelujah" was book-ended by laughter. A couple people were dancing like gypsies for some reason. This was all going across my movie screen, a little surreal to be sure, but also quite refreshing.

Gradually something started to change in the atmosphere. I began to get a growing sense of things beginning to lead somewhere in the conversation. Some organizational vibes started to buzz around, as folks slowly started to pack stuff up. Jesse, the guy with the eyes who had led me in prayer, began to indicate that this new beginning was actually the new beginning of something rather specific. A little "uh-oh" began to arise in my spirit, like the feeling you get when you realize that the smiling, friendly person you've been chatting with is actually selling something. My defense system began to come alive, as well as thoughts of my girlfriend on the other seaboard and my dreams, vague though they were, of exploring life on my own for a while. My sense of balance, as teeter tottering as it was, made me want to step back and digest all this a bit. "Why don't I come down and see you guys at your commune in LA in a few days?" I said.

This clearly wouldn't do. Jesse's eyes began to focus sharply again. I had made the mistake of telling him about my search for Jesus, and that dotted line I'd signed with God on the beach that morning. Jesse actually grabbed me by the arm and locked my gaze back into his and pronounced with all the authority of a messenger sent straight from God, "You can't say a prayer like that in the morning, then come face to face with more truth than you've ever seen in your whole life that afternoon, and then just walk away. You *know* you're supposed to be with us. If you walk away now you'll never be able to tell yourself you're seeking the truth again, and frankly, I believe you'll just go *crazy!*"

My insides turned to Jell-O. I could picture my future devolve into insanity, envisioning stumbling down the street mumbling to myself, a bottle of Wild Irish Rose in a brown paper sack dangling from one hand. Geez...I damned well better get on this bus! I told Jesse I'd be back soon and ran breathlessly back to Bill's apartment to grab my knapsack. As I dashed out the door Bill and some friends were seated cross-legged about a coffee table passing around a water pipe. He looked up and in a very mellow tone asked me where I was headed. "I'm going to follow Jesus!" I replied. "Gotta run!" A strange quiet fell. Someone started coughing on their last toke. Bill spoke up, rather graciously I thought: "Jesus is cool, man." I realized he meant probably not quite as cool as Krishnamurti, but still passably cool. "Yeah, he is!" I said. "I'll be in touch!" And off I ran.

As I got back to the encampment, the big yellow bus in which the group traveled already had its diesel engine humming. Small clusters of Jesus revolutionaries milled about. Some were conversing excitedly with new converts who were getting ready to come aboard for the Jesus journey. Others, having put off the decision, were getting as much exhortation as their somewhat disappointed counselors could possibly squeeze in, maybe a quick overview of the prophetic time line of the world's future, or a warning about the Great Whore Babylon that was seducing the planet. Jesse spotted me, and with a relief that only slightly eased his seriousness, began to usher me towards the door of the bus.

There we were met by a very imposing figure, well over six feet and built like a biker, wearing wraparound shades, sporting a heavy two-day growth of beard and a militant-looking beret. "He wants to follow Jesus, Josh," Jesse said, as though it were a password to get me on board. Josh stared down even more intensely than Jesse, searching my eyes. "So, are you ready to *die* for Jesus?" he challenged. I was dumbstruck. What did he mean? Right now? I wondered. Jesse piped in: "He just got saved, Josh, but he wants to give it a try." I was actually beginning to wonder myself, as Josh studied me for a few more moments. He finally let me pass, though it did seem he had some reservations. I felt like I'd barely escaped the "sorry, Charlie" rejection of Starkist tuna ad fame. I boarded the bus bound for the unknown, being drawn along by a force I really couldn't explain.

My eyes tried to take in the scene. A motley crew if there ever was one, and me feeling at least as motley as the rest. But soon we were rolling towards LA singing (I *never* sang!) "Oh Happy Day," over and over, listening to people give their testimonies. (My religious vocabulary was beginning to expand.) I remember Josh handing me the microphone to testify. I mumbled something about having "thought Jesus was a character in a J.D. Salinger novel." My comments were met with somewhat puzzled stares. Embarrassed, I passed the mic back to Josh, who clearly was making a note to self to talk a little more with Jesse about this guy, as he quickly segued into a spirited chorus of "I have decided to follow Jesus!" just to clear the air of any spirit of confusion I'd invited on board. On we traveled into the night.

CHAPTER 3

DOWN THE RABBIT HOLE

....*this time she found a little bottle on it ("which certainly was not here before," said Alice,) and tied round the neck of the bottle was a paper label, with the words "DRINK ME" beautifully printed on it in large letters.*

It was all very well to say, "Drink me," but the wise little Alice was not going to do that *in a hurry. "No, I'll look first," she said, "and see whether it's marked* poison *or not," for she had read several nice little stories about children who had got burnt, and eaten up by wild beasts, and other unpleasant things, all because they* would *not remember the simple rules their friends had taught them: such as, that a red-hot poker will burn you if you hold it too long; and she had never forgotten that if you drink much from a bottle marked "poison," it is almost certain to disagree with you, sooner or later.*

However, this bottle was not *marked "poison," so Alice ventured to taste it, and finding it very nice (it had, in fact, a sort of mixed flavor of cherry-tart, custard, pine-apple, roast turkey, taffy, and hot-buttered toast,) she very soon finished it off.*

"What a curious feeling!" said Alice. "I must be shutting up like a telescope."[2]

~ Lewis Carroll, *Alice in Wonderland*

The commune turned out to be a five-story building located in the scenic skid row district of downtown Los Angeles. We were hustled past a handful of brown bag wine tasters who were gathered by the mission awaiting some free food as we entered into another world. The décor was 1950s mission, with scriptures on the wall and a huge black-and-white portrait of Jesus hung ceiling to floor. Some team members scurried thither and yon putting away props from the vigil, while others readied for an evening snack of donated butter brickle ice cream, served from huge tubs into individual serving bowls that seemed big enough to serve a fair size family. More testimonies and songs, and then the other new recruits and I, already physically and emotionally exhausted to the point of a mind-altering state, were ushered upstairs to what I later learned was affectionately called "the second floor purge room."

If my experience earlier that day was being born again, then I guess what transpired in that room was like the doctor picking up the baby by the heels and smacking his bottom to welcome him into the new world. What followed were several hours of "good cop/bad cop" style ministry. We were alternately offered encouragement for having given our hearts to Jesus, and then were treated to an intensely melodramatic illustrated sermon on the dire consequences of "backsliding" (what on earth was that?) The speaker shouted that we would be "crucifying the Son of God afresh," slamming his fist into the wall to signify driving the nails through Jesus' hands again if we should turn our backs on Him. In retrospect, this was clearly a bit heavy for a believer still so wet behind the ears. Some new recruits had second thoughts, gathering their things and half slinking, half hightailing it out the door back to "the pit." We who remained, however, were now initiated into the Revolution. Being shown to a bunk, I collapsed, unable to even begin to take stock of things in any rational fashion.

The morning arrived with a guitar strumming reveille, lots of "hallelujahs" and "praise the Lords" filling the air, as if to exorcise any demons that might have tried to weasel in during the night.

It seemed like everything was permanently set on volume 10. I was trying to bring order to my internal voices through all this, fighting to stay focused on this new world enveloping me. But midway through my first "babes class" on the topic of the Word, my mind started drifting to thoughts of my girlfriend back east. I was wishing I could sit and share all this input with her, partly to see her "saved" and partly to see if I could even begin to coherently explain any of it at all. I think a few other "babes" might have been meditating on things other than the Word as well, as our teacher abruptly stopped and with 100 percent conviction and all the aplomb of a Marine drill sergeant shouted out, "Anything you are thinking about right now that is NOT the WORD OF GOD is the DEVIL!"

As this seemed to echo off the institutional green high gloss walls, voices began to come alive in my mind: "You were thinking about Ginny! He just called Ginny the devil! That's it! I'm outta here!" And I stood up and walked out of the room, headed to my bunk to collect my backpack, taking time to fish Ginny's high school graduation picture from my stuff. So armed, I started walking towards the exit, the picture in hand. An "older brother" met me in the hall and asked me where I was going, clearly concerned for my soul. I stopped, held Ginny's picture up to his face, and shouted, "DOES *THAT* LOOK LIKE THE *DEVIL* TO YOU?"

He was obviously puzzled by the question and gently suggested we sit and talk a bit. He counseled me for a half hour or so, assuring me that my logic had skipped a few steps and that God loved Ginny more than I did. He prayed with me for her eternal salvation and promised to help me write her a letter explaining God's plan from the Bible. He went on to hint that they were hoping to send a team to the East Coast soon, and I would be a likely candidate to join the mission. He encouraged me to get strong in the Lord so God could use me to reach my loved ones. He gave me two scriptures to memorize: "Trust in the Lord with all thine heart, and lean not unto thine own understanding" (Proverbs 3:5) and "Delight thyself also in the Lord, and He shall give thee the desires of thine heart" (Psalm 37:4).

If you are thinking that this was a manipulative way to use scripture on me to channel me back into the fold, I will have to agree with you. But you know, I found some amazing power in memorizing these scriptures, as well as the hundreds more I would learn in the days that followed. A little hard to explain, but that's life—at least *my* life!

The next few weeks were a whirl of experiences, a torrent of biblical information, one long prayer meeting/worship service with only brief interruptions to do things I would never have imagined myself doing. I remember having to shave my beard and get my hair cut by someone who clearly hated the concept of symmetry. They were "idols," I was told, and that was probably true. I remember being bussed to a television studio where the set consisted of a cardboard church backdrop complete with colored cellophane stained glass windows. We were to help in the recording of an early version of TV evangelism, produced by an independent minister who was our main sponsor at the time. This scene did touch off some murmuring amongst the ex-bikers and hippies, which was soon silenced by a talk on being revolutionary enough to not appear revolutionary, and how this would help us conquer the world and avoid the draft simultaneously. That brought a few exclamations of "Amen, brother!"

The group had adopted the name "The Children of God," after having been labeled that by a reporter who saw a parallel with the Children of Israel of old. To help us along the road to our new lives, we were each also given a new name taken from the Bible. From now on I was to be known as Kenaz. This was not due to any special revelation, but simply that the new recruits in my class were all getting names pulled from the same genealogy in I Chronicles. Things could have been worse. At least it wasn't Shuhite or Buzi, and I guess Kenaz did have sort of a Middle Earth ring to it.

Next I was introduced to street evangelism. It was almost an out-of-body experience to observe myself stopping strangers on the streets of downtown LA to ask them if had ever met the Lord. It was really out of character for me, but we had learned that this was the work of a disciple, and if we were ashamed of Him before men, He would be ashamed of us when we stood before Him. Hi-ho! Hi-ho! It's off to work we go.

But things really got rolling for me when a week or so later I was selected to go with a busload of other new recruits for training in Texas at our other big "colony," the meaning-laden term we used for our communities, which we envisioned eventually colonizing the planet. For the uninitiated, "The Ranch in Texas" was a highly euphemistic expression referring to an incredibly barren patch of reddish, dusty earth in the middle of nowhere with a few groves of mesquite thorn trees scattered about. Mesquite branches, it turned out, made great building material for the security fences we were erecting around the perimeter of our little promised land. These were to protect us from enemies such as "the Romans" (i.e., a biblical allusion meaning the police) or "Chariots out of Assyria"—I kid you not—this referred to pickup trucks visible from the dust cloud approaching from the north, possibly containing drunken cowboys hunting for hippies and Jesus freaks. And of course. we were constantly on the lookout for the always risky "Pharisees" (church people) who might arrive to "spy out our liberty."

The campus was populated by a few rows of bunkhouses that could house a "tribe" of about ten revolutionaries on rusty metal bunks and thin cotton mattresses that had a sort of archeological scent about them. There also was a large cinder block mess hall that sported in massive letters on the roof "JESUS LOVES YOU" as a witness to helicopter pilots training at a nearby military base. Some of these guys would land, possibly for the hugs from the sisters—our "revolutionary women" seldom wore bras. Amazingly enough, many of the pilots prayed to accept Christ, and at least one eventually joined. Witnessing opportunities were rare in our location about a million miles from the nearest truck stop, so it was really dangerous for any unsaved within shouting distance of several hundred zealots. We each had memorized five or ten Bible verses that day, and were anxious to "sharpen our swords," as we used to refer to these adventures in evangelism, utterly without embarrassment.

On the grounds there were a few more conventional bungalows that housed the babies and kids and some leadership couples. There were also a few scattered school buses and antiquated camping trailers, and off by itself, in a no-trespassing zone, an old Dodge motor home referred to as the Ark—where the mysterious "Moses" lived—but more on that later.

It was an utterly amazing fact that somehow forces beyond our control seemed to have collected this menagerie of dopers and drill sergeants, bikers and Baptists, draft dodgers and artful-dodgers, hookers and holy rollers, all now wearing cowboy hats and cutoffs or granny dresses and combat boots, and all sporting index cards with memory verses from the book of Revelation, or perhaps Ezekiel, dangling from a clip on a string hung around their necks. We sang and thanked the Lord for the food for fifteen to twenty minutes before dining on something called milo, a cereal normally sold as chickenfeed, and donated day-old donuts. Then we sang some more and hugged and danced in a circle until we all had acid grins threatening to permanently crease our young idealistic cheeks. When some thought from my previous existence crept into my consciousness, like *What the heck am I doing here?* all I needed to do was look over at this black jazz musician hugging the tattooed low rider, and I would be snapped back into my new reality. This *must* be some sort of miracle preparing the way for Christ's return!

What was going on here was a collective "wilderness experience." Old identities were being shed, and new creatures in Christ Jesus were coming into existence. Our physical condition was pretty appalling. I remember the experience of trying to shave—an abomination in itself to my previous personality—with a rusty razor blade that seemed to have been left over from some World War II surplus depot. I recall standing around an outdoor spigot with a group of other fellows, each of us attempting to lather up with a small piece of a mini soap bar from some bankrupt motel, while I searching for an image of my chin in a black-flecked shard of a broken mirror. And then there was hunting for an always hard to find pair of size 12 shoes in the "Free Store" to replace my boots, which now had a detached sole that flopped when I walked, like a tongue hanging out of the mouth of a stray dog. I will never forget the sunburn on the back of my newly exposed Irish neck that had long been protected by hippie hair. It was seriously blistered and itched so badly it made me want to cry. And after all that there was also the challenge of enduring a prophecy class on the Last Seven Years for the umpteenth time from a guy who habitually picked his nose. Charming.

But I can also remember soaking in the Bible. We had three to four hours of intense group Bible studies, and memorized scriptures during every other activity of the day, such as planting a watermelon patch in dirt so dry the Johnson grass was brown—talk about otherworldly! Then we would relax at night watching black-and-white filmstrips called *The Bible in Pictures*. They were so ancient they appeared to be actual photographs taken at the original battle of Jericho. And we loved it! Even after all that I remember drinking two large glasses of water before bedtime so that nature's call would awaken me just before dawn. This was so I could get up for an hour or two of uninterrupted Bible reading *before* morning devotions with my tribe. And I was still waiting anxiously for our Sunday free day to arrive so I could go off under a mesquite tree and read through the Epistles of Paul in one sitting. Whether you view four months of this from a perspective of a Bible believing Christian or a behavioral psychologist (or both!), it is not hard to see that some serious reorientation of my internal map was well underway.

And let's not forget prayer. Man, did we pray! In one of her books writer Anne Lamott describes an elderly black saint from down South who, when she prayed, would look "as if she's holding the whole earth together, and making the biggest wish in the world."[3] Well, that sister may have come off as a little bit lukewarm in one of our prayer meetings. I remember kneeling in a circle on the cement floor at our tribe meeting with our faces buried in our hands and foreheads touching the floor almost Muslim-style, and crying out to God with all that was within us. We sought God for everything from the salvation of our loved ones to the needs of the camp to be dropped out of heaven to asking Him to mercifully throw our poor benighted brother who had backslidden that day into jail so that he could come to his senses before it was too late and he'd have to enter into an eternity of everlasting shame and contempt. Thank the Lord that the gift of calling fire down out of heaven wasn't doled out with the gift of tongues, or I fear there would be little left of the military-industrial complex, the educational system, or most of the major denominations, for that matter.

Moses spent forty years tending sheep on the "back side of the desert." John the Baptist spent years in the wilderness like his forefather Elijah, clothed in camel's hair and eating locusts and wild honey when he was lucky enough to get it. Jesus even spent forty days fasting in the wilderness before launching his public ministry. And the Children of God had the Texas Soul Clinic somewhere between Thurber and Mingus several miles off State Route 180, and a "180" we did!

Another feature in our patented forty-day wilderness makeover was learning to yield and obey. Regimentation was not high on the list of favorite things of most children of the sixties, but it was key to the character of a spiritual revolutionary and *this* was boot camp. Schedules were more abundant than at a preschool day camp. Everyone had a "buddy" who was virtually omnipresent to help each other stay on the straight and narrow. There were rules for everything from how to do the dishes to how many sheets of toilet paper a revolutionary could use. This latter rule was reinforced with a reminder posted next to the dispenser: "The eyes of the Lord are in every place, beholding the evil and the good" (Proverbs 15:3). "Rebellion" or "murmuring" would be met with a drastic passage from the book of Numbers about the earth swallowing the enemies of Moses, or quail being regurgitated through the nostrils of the ungrateful Children of Israel. In retrospect, it seems rather amazing that so many of us stuck around through all this. But, really, who wanted to have to face God at the Great White Throne and explain that he had deserted his post in the Last Days Army over the toilet tissue issue? (Ramping up the trivial tended to distract from the weightier issues of loss of personal freedom, etc. Strain at gnats, swallow camels.)

The Gandalf—or perhaps, as it turned out, Saruman—figure of this entire Middle Earth community was rarely seen and was spoken of only in somewhat hushed tones. The Moses of our new Israel was a defrocked former pastor of a rural Christian and Missionary Alliance church, David Berg (a.k.a. Mo and/or Dad.) As babes in Los Angeles we'd heard about this dude (it was LA, remember) that was rumored to be so in tune with God that he could "look into your eyes and see all your sins." It was said that because of this he always wore sunglasses, even at night, so as not to totally freak out the newcomers. While at the ranch we would occasionally have the "blessing" of Mo's personal presence at special meetings. No one tried to explain about the much younger lady who was always at his side and lived with him in that motor home nicknamed "the Ark" that I spoke about. Strangely, it did not seem to raise any eyebrows. The explanation for all that would come later, but during my Soul Clinic sojourn, I did get to catch Mo's act as he delivered some memorable sermons that would eventually become *Mo Letters*, the new foundational teachings for the movement as it evolved over the years to come.

It's hard to say what I would have thought upon meeting this man if the stage had not been set as thoroughly as it had been. I was just shy of twenty, had passed through the generational disillusionment of the sixties, and had focused intensely on an utterly sincere spiritual search climaxing in a powerful personal conversion. I was now experiencing a total immersion baptism into a radical biblical worldview in a massively reinforcing environment. All those I trusted to guide me spiritually were clearly utterly loyal and somewhat in awe of Mo. He carried himself with a swagger of spiritual authority unlike anything I'd ever been exposed to before. His manner just sort of grabbed you and made you sit up and take notice— serious notice. There was a sense that what you were about to hear was a privilege few were ever granted...and your ability to "drink it in" would clearly impact your effectiveness in God's new revolution.

Plus, there was a sort of hip, Black Pantherishness about the "right ons" and "preach it, brothers" the older brethren shouted out. It all made some kind of perfect sixties revolutionary sense. In our collective and individual psyches we were taking one more step on the journey to the Promised Land.

And now it was time to go out into all the world and make disciples of all nations, beginning with Cincinnati.

CHAPTER 4

NUMBERS AND EXODUS

We're pirates, we're pirates
We're gospel gypsy pirates
We're sailing, we're sailing,
O'er uncharted seas.

~ *COG Song by Aaron Berg*

Over the next few years, the Children of God experienced explosive numerical growth and rapid decentralization, scattering into many cities throughout the US and overseas as well. We quickly gained notoriety as the "storm troopers of the Jesus movement," a title *TIME* magazine bestowed upon us. We were on our way to colonize the world and reap the harvest before the Lord's impending return. No one could accuse us of thinking small back then.

In one of the early pioneer ventures, during the autumn of 1970, a team was sent up from Texas to take over an independent Jesus House near the University of Cincinnati, as well as to setup a nearby "babes ranch" in Kentucky. (Lest you get the wrong idea, "babes ranch" refers to a rural training center for new recruits.) The Kentucky Farm, as it became known, was actually a two-room clapboard cabin with a potbellied stove and no plumbing of any type. Local hillbillies actually felt sorry for us.

Due to various factors I was chosen for the team, which thrilled me. Although I had forsaken them for the Lord, I was still harboring hope that my girlfriend and a few other close friends back East might see the light, burn their bridges, and join the Revolution. I was still clinging to that verse I had memorized back on Day One: "Delight thyself also in the Lord, and He shall give thee the desires of thine heart."

But as the movement expanded, and I graduated from "babe" to "leadership trainee," my conversion into "Kenaz Acts" became more complete. (The surname "Acts" was added, as I had now become a Bible teacher with a specialization in "The Acts of the Apostles.") Life was full of witnessing, Bible study, prayer, worship, and now leadership training. This last item consisted of the privileged reading of *Mo Letters* from our now world-traveling guru on everything from prophetic interpretation of current events to biblical tips on love-making to the importance of using onionskin paper in international correspondence to save on postage. Oddly, this last item received more detailed coverage than many prophetic events.

I began to share a growing responsibility for the well-being of the flock, caring first for a younger buddy, then a small tribe, and eventually as a sort of associate pastor of this colony. Within a few months the house held a seam-busting sixty or so people—not counting the ones we'd shipped to the Kentucky farm for indoctrination. We had been nationally televised by NBC in an enthusiastic, if somewhat skewed documentary called *The Ultimate Trip*. Each week we prayed with hundreds of kids on the street to receive Jesus, and usually a few dropped out to become disciples. We had all kinds of excitement from "10:36ers," an expression we used to describe hostile parents, taken from the Bible verse Matthew 10:36, warning that "A man's foes shall be they of his own household." These would occasionally storm the front door with loaded weapons!

Popular rock musicians were joining. We rejoiced at news of new pioneer teams shooting out all over the continent and preparing to go overseas. And we were amazed at the miracle of God providing our needs in sometimes wildly unorthodox ways, ranging from donations of goods from local businesses to the savings of new disciples put into the common pot to anonymous gifts left under windshield wipers of our vehicle. Specific needs were often met through perfectly timed coincidences in answer to prayer, or even through guidance in dreams and visions. We were intoxicated with a sense of having somehow tapped into a rich, undiscovered vein of the Creator's power source, and we were all drinking from a fire hose. Though I ached for my loved ones from my old life, my new life was clearly gathering steam, and I rejoiced to recognize my own ongoing transformation.

A few things happened during this period that were an indication of just how much I had changed. Right around Christmas that year, due to my parents' home being close to New York City, I was part of a team that was sent to collect the car that Mo had left in the JFK Airport's long-term parking lot when he departed on his now historic trip to Europe. During the visit, I somehow managed to cajole about a dozen of my closest friends to gather in my parents' living room to share my testimony with them. They got not only that, but also an overview of the entire sweep of Bible prophecy, including a clear understanding of why they should dropout and "quit f—king the Great Whore Babylon." I was puzzled and troubled by their lack of willingness to immediately leave their nets and follow the Master. But I did thank the Lord for a chance to deliver my soul. Their blood would no longer be on my hands—a phrase taken from Ezekiel Chapter 3, which upon reflection really should have disturbed me way more than it did. Though troubled at the time, I somehow managed to set aside my concerns and move on to more urgent matters of world conquest.

Within a few months I had to once again return to New Jersey, this time alone (a great test, as I was solemnly warned) for my draft board hearing. The board members were Catholic, and one of them was the very conservative father of a close friend of mine who had recently gotten saved and was herself veering dangerously towards "the sect" and was already at least partly, horror of horrors, Protestant. So it was no great surprise that my petition for a ministerial deferment was denied. (I was later determined unfit to serve in an almost "Alice's Restaurant" length saga at my draft physical, but I'll spare you the details.) But I remained unwavering in my loyalty to the Revolution for Jesus, and even hooked my youngest (sixteen-year-old) brother into starting the first "catacombs colony," a group of kids that met in our parents' basement for several years until he was old enough to join full-time. I was an on-fire brother, and with new colonies opening up all the time, I came to be viewed as a potential new shepherd. I just needed to find "a little wifey," as we used to affectionately refer to our better halves.

Courtship in the Family was, shall we say, a little different from the cultural norm. An anthropologist would have a field day with the mating habits of the Children of God, and there are as many anomalies as there are stories. As it is so highly integral to this account, I'll try to quickly summarize our little romantic comedy.

As mentioned, the need of the hour was for married couples to lead colonies. As an up-and-coming young leader, it was pointed out to me that it was my time. I was somewhat ambivalent about this, as I saw that many married couples on the team dissolved into cycles of marriage squabbles that were not only uncomfortable to watch at close quarters, but also destroyed their usefulness to the Kingdom. We were supposed to radiate joy. People having serious marriage problems just couldn't sell God very effectively. Nevertheless, I nervously decided to fulfill my responsibility to the community for the sake of the Great Commission.

The problem was that there were only three or four single women in the colony and roughly thirty or so single men. However, as part of our plan to deal with draft boards, the Children of God were having a mass ordination ceremony at the LA mission building. It was pointed out to me that there were many single girls at the Ranch in Texas (which we would pass through) and in LA, and that should enable me return with a wife. The fact that I did not actually know any of these young ladies seemed to present little problem, as we all knew God could do miracles, though I personally wondered about some of the "miracle marriages" I had been observing so far.

Now I was forced to finally admit that I sorta kinda thought I might be sensing the Lord's leading towards one of those few sisters there in Cincy, Hodiah Preacherwoman. Hodiah had joined the same day that I had at the Jerry Rubin rally in Santa Barbara. She'd been a hitchhiking hippie en route to Big Sur, whose ride had stopped in town to score some grass. I had noticed her then, originally thinking I ought to try and speak with her to see what she was thinking about this whole scene, but we next met in the LA second-floor purge room, where such a conversation would have been decidedly out of place.

She became a featured interviewee at the cardboard church TV show, which is where she earned her nickname. The televangelist, Fred Jordan, had a hard time getting the microphone back from her as she started going a little overboard, exhorting viewers on the biblical injunction to "forsake all." This message wasn't exactly geared for the housebound geriatrics that so enjoyed the testimonies of these young dope addicts coming to the Lord and that were also generously financing Fred's rather unRevolutionary lifestyle out of appreciation. Thereafter, she had been dubbed "Preacherwoman."

She really started to get my attention when we crossed paths at the Ranch while peeling potatoes or doing dishes. I was impressed by her prodigious command of the Scripture Memory Card, far more than her wild Janis Joplin hairdo and demeanor, or even her unique cutoffs-with-combat-boots couture, as attractive as that was. A solid memory system seemed a fine quality in a revolutionary woman, a fact I quietly stored away for future reference. Well, that future had arrived, and I screwed up all my courage and approached my leaders, expressing my hesitancy to return with a wife, as I kinda sorta thought maybe the Lord was leading, etc., etc. "Good thing you said something," the shepherd replied, "two other guys have asked to marry her...so this is a new factor we will pray about." Well, that would be a good test, I decided, and at least I'd still be single when I got back from LA.

Long story short, after several months and some personnel shuffles, we both ended up in Cincy again at the same time. I was coaxed to finally propose, which happened on a winding staircase with some married sisters listening in from above—not a real Kodak moment, I'm afraid. How did Hodiah respond? "What does leadership have to say?" Again, not exactly Meg Ryan and Tom Hanks stuff. But at least I could report back and see if the pinball would magically wind its way into the match zone, and bells would ring.

A few weeks later, while we were on a witnessing trip to a pop festival, we had a combination inspiration/outreach and betrothal. This was followed by marriage in a few more weeks, during which we utterly destroyed our parents with phone calls to simultaneously share the happy news, and request our birth certificates by return mail. This was not exactly proper etiquette, I was to learn over the next twenty or so years.

After catching a ride with the team designated to collect donated goods, we were married across the river in scenic Newport, Kentucky, where we met the minimum age requirement. We had a less than stirring ceremony with a justice of the peace, complete with snapshots in front of the American flag and the well-known "praying hands" icon, just so we could prove to people we were really married. The honeymoon consisted of an afternoon and evening off, a bottle of Manechevitz wine, and a private bedroom. (We'd be moving into shared quarters with another couple the next day with only a makeshift curtain between us for privacy.)

Now hitched, our career took off shepherding homes in Atlanta, and pioneering Norfolk, Virginia, where I eventually delivered our first son, Jubilee, under circumstances that would easily be worth ten thousand dollars on *America's Funniest Home Videos*, if we'd shot one. We were experiencing some amazing answers to prayer, which continually reinforced our sense of calling. Then came a tragedy that would deepen our commitment to the cause even further.

Through a series of strange coincidences in response to specific prayers, we ended up receiving a backslidden brother, James, back into the fold. He was a zealous soul winner, telling just about every doggone human being who happened to be within ten feet of him about the Lord. Yet he'd backslidden several times over issues such as really wanting a Big Mac, only to return in a few weeks or months with a flock of new believers in tow. We deeply loved this brother despite his somewhat conflicted soul. In another series of coincidences we ended up singing in a park one Sunday afternoon when without warning James was tragically stabbed in the back by a total stranger.

Another brother and I followed the ambulance to the hospital, where after several hours of keeping vigil, we were informed that James had died. Returning to the house and gathering the handful of young believers to share this news was extremely difficult, but also deeply impacting. Amid many tears, we all sought the Lord for the grace to die as martyrs. In the way a cowboy wants to die with his boots on, we wanted to go with the name of Jesus on our lips, as our dear brother James had that day.

Over the next year and a half, we became regional shepherds responsible for up to twenty colonies in the Northeast and Midwest. Reflecting back upon this, it seems to me a little unbelievable. We were just kids, barely twenty years old, for heaven's sake! We were newly married, with no premarital preparation, and fumbling our way through those adjustments in the pressure cooker of a communal setting. Our preparedness for parenting was strictly what had been passed down to us through our experiences in our families of origin and our genetic instincts. During this period we were also to have our second child. Thank God we at least had a self-taught midwife present for that one! Our theological training, though Bible intensive, was decidedly haphazard. And as far as management or counseling skills go, I shudder to think of the template we were operating from. Now here we were shepherding over two hundred fresh-off-the-street young believers, in twenty locations, spread over a dozen states. Yowee. But we were now considered leaders in the movement, which served to further cement our new identities.

Then, in the fall of 1973, Mo received a cryptic revelation that seemed to indicate that the comet Kohoutek, due in December of that year, foretold the impending fall of the United States. (In classic prophetic form, he would later claim to have been misinterpreted. Naturally.) This prompted a massive migration of misguided missionaries into all the world, partly to save the lost and partly to escape ourselves from the wrath soon to come. Within a few months—after some dreams, signs, coincidences of supply, and a few brief exchanges of letters—we gathered together our meager belongings and enough cloth diapers to keep our two boys supplied, and off we flew to join a pioneer team to India.

Over the next few years we bounced around leadership positions in India, England, and eventually an area that stretched from Greece all the way to Bangladesh. We were also involved in pioneer efforts to such danger zones as Iran, Pakistan, and the Persian Gulf States. We could fill many chapters with stories of a rollercoaster life of joys, hardships, miracles, frustrations, dramatic deliverances, and foolhardy failures. All the while, we continued having babies, close calls with various authorities, and experiencing the wonders of living an impossible life in impossible lands, with an impossibly faith-walking group of committed and often comical zealots. Thinking back on those days makes me laugh, cry, shake my head in disbelief, and want to invite a whole list of amazing friends over for a meal of fresh chapattis and dhal at some roadside stand that would cause the average US health official to go ballistic. We did some wild things and were foolish beyond belief, but a lot of people were introduced to lasting relationships with Jesus, despite our scrambled theology. I'm sure there were many emotional casualties along the way, but we were utterly oblivious to it at the time. What sticks in our memories are some of the funniest scenes I ever experienced unfolding around us on a weekly basis. We found ourselves living practically naked on hippie beaches while guests of the Jesuits in Goa, becoming friends with Bollywood film stars, being chased by immigration authorities, producing radio and stage shows, and encountering a cast of characters even Fellini could not have imagined. Through it all, our commitment to the movement had grown virtually unshakable.

Yet on another level, the movement, which had always been clearly out of sync with anything remotely mainstream, was charting new pathways in the wilderness of weird. Most of us had long since mastered the art of managing cognitive dissonance—the ability of the mind to hold two conflicting concepts at the same time. In addition to Mo's diatribes against the system and long exhortations to faithfulness, he was also given to strange dreams about goddesses and aliens. He was convinced that characters from works of fiction such as *Don Quixote* and *Heidi* were actual spirit beings counseling him from beyond the veil. In fact, it seemed that a rather large chunk of his consciousness had taken up permanent residence on "the other side," which we later came to discover was also heavily littered with empty sherry bottles, a key ingredient in his mystical alchemy. We'd all try and take this stuff in on some level, try to extract some little hint of bearing it might have in some oblique way on our own projects, and then we'd get back to the everyday issues of survival and into the work we believed that we were building for the Lord.

But now a new series of revelations was clearly something more and was leading toward a major paradigm shift for the movement. This new turn was to impact us all in so many ways it would be difficult to track them all down. Mo was about to go public with a new sexual revolution. His vision was a watershed of bad ideas, which clearly the biblical writers had universally rejected. But at our prophet's leading, we proceeded to pry open this Pandora's box. Its impact upon our own lives, those of our converts, and most importantly on our children would serve to remind all who had eyes to see why, as Jesus once said, "from the beginning it was not so."

CHAPTER 5

THE PLOT THICKENS

So many fantastic colors: I feel in a wonderland.
Many fantastic colors, makes me feel so good.
You've got that pure feel, such good responses.
You've got that rainbow feel, but the rainbow has a beard.

~ Jack Bruce and Pete Brown (of Cream), "SWLABR"

Probably the most pivotal point in the Family's wild history was the introduction of that headline-making doctrinal/social experiment known as Flirty Fishing (a.k.a. FFing—which I will try and explain below) and the sexual revolution that followed. For years the Family (as the group had gradually come to called) had been known for its quirky teachings nibbling at the edges of sexual liberation. Mo published and we widely distributed tracts such as "C'mon Ma, Burn Your Bra," "Revolutionary Women," and the oft-cited "Mountain Maid" with its combination of junior high level rhyming and double entendre. Up until then, though, other than the use of relatively mild forms of flirtatious sex appeal as a sort of "sales tool" while witnessing, sex outside of marriage was a definite no-no. (We were soon to find out that exceptions applied for Mo and a few inner circle leaders.)

Behind the scenes, Mo and his younger secretary/second wife Maria had begun a distinctly wilder after-hours ministry to lonely hearts, first in London, and then later with amazing boldness on the Spanish resort island of Tenerife. (By the way, this was the same very attentive younger lady who had lived with Mo in the motor home back at the Ranch. She had been given "prophetically" to Mo as a symbol of God's new bride... replacing the cold and infertile church. Seemed a little convenient, I know, but stuff like this barely raised a ripple amongst the faithful.) The concept behind this new tactic was based on Mo's conviction that sex was a gift from God and beautiful when shared in a spirit of love, regardless of one's marital status. In this vein, Mo taught that under certain circumstances it could be a way of physically expressing God's love, in the same way that caring for the physical needs of the sick and hungry was. This idea was eventually developed into a rather elaborate doctrine he called "The Law of Love." He used scriptures intended to contrast Old Testament emphasis on "keeping the law" with the New Testament's message of freedom from legalism. "All things are lawful," the Apostle says, when we are "led by the Spirit" and motivated by Love. If one ignores the original context and language, and doesn't pay very close attention to definitions, it is not hard to see how this could lead to a pretty permissive interpretative system.

Mo and Maria and a few others began experimenting with this new "witnessing method" pretty aggressively. All was recorded in lurid detail that would rival *Letters to Penthouse* and would later be published as a sort of how-to manual for the rest of the Family. When they finally spilled the beans on this newest revelation, the reaction was mixed. Although a significant number of disciples departed, surprisingly, most of us followed on. This acceptance was accompanied with varying levels of fear, reluctance, enthusiasm, and marital meltdown, along with the usual reformatting of large areas of the brain. The unfolding of this doctrine and the introduction of its soon to follow relative, "sharing," would have major ramifications for the movement. It ensured an even more dramatic alienation from the orthodox Christian community. Most significantly, in the long run, was the reengineering of the nuclear family, which was already highly unstable due to communal pressures and abusive authoritarian interference.

A string of *Mo Letters* such as "To FF or Not to FF" and "Doubts" were published and assigned on special reading lists designed to get the "slow of heart to believe" on board. The ideas presented in this disastrous experiment were so contrary to society's normal attitudes towards marriage and sex, as well as the common understanding of the Bible's teaching on the subject, that it took some pretty hard pressing down on the needle here to create new grooves in the record. No one came out the other side of this without some dramatically rearranged thought patterns.

The many issues involved in this ultimately very destructive practice have been exposed at length in journalistic accounts of the Family's sexual revolution around the world. All of this affected us in many ways, but for the purpose of this narrative, I want to skip to the impact this new turn had on the structure of the Family as a movement, and move on to how it resulted in a dramatic move to a more centralized, more tightly controlled organization. I'll also touch on its radical reshaping of my own personal family.

As mentioned, Mo and Maria and their personal staff had spent several years in a self-imposed virtual exile while they "pioneered" FFing in London and the Canary Islands. During this period they left much of the administration and overall direction of the work to various regional leaders, who often tended to build their own kingdoms, straying somewhat from the spirit and vision of Mo, which many of them found impractical and counterproductive. "Spirit trips" don't really pay the bills or enlarge the borders of one's domain, and they are a real pain in the butt to try and explain to the press. Some of these regional leaders were themselves quite abusive and manipulative, but usually in the more pedestrian matters of power, pride, greed, and lust, without the more exotic spiritualistic stuff thrown in. The stage was being set for a confrontation: Moses off on the mountaintop getting the new revelation from God, while his designated Aaronic leaders were creating their own idols from the people's gold.

When Mo decided to roll out his new marketing plan to the sales force worldwide, he encountered an uneven response. Not only were the new teachings sometimes balked at, but he also encountered a measure of resistance from some leaders whom he sensed might have preferred if he stayed on his mountaintop and left managing the fiefdoms to them. After wrestling with piecemeal solutions for a while, he finally blew up and fired the entire "chain of command." For pragmatic reasons he did cut some inside deals with some of the most senior leaders, including his own children and their spouses, allowing them to continue temporarily in some comfortable position, rather than having to deal with the possibility of a destabilizing mass exodus at that time.

After a period of some chaos in the late seventies, what reasserted itself was a far more centralized administrative structure, with more unquestioningly loyal, pliable, and generally less independent personalities in leadership positions. Mo adopted a more Machiavellian approach, keeping the reins more tightly in his own hands and those of his second wife, Maria, along with a few of their closest staff. As the movement was scattered all around the world, various areas still had differing attitudes and localized cultures to some extent. With this reorganization the days of rival kingdoms was fast disappearing, along with those that had led them. Most of these leaders eventually drifted out of the movement over the next few years.

How all this impacted my personal family is another matter. India and the Middle East were never considered much of a prized plum. One very senior Europe-based leader actually preferred to have the area removed from her oversight rather than to have to visit "that dirty place." But someone had to supervise it somehow. For a variety of reasons, some of which I may not even know, we were selected to oversee the area from Greece to Bangladesh, as well as much of Africa for awhile.

THE PLOT THICKENS

One little twist to all new appointments was a feature designed to balance out the overly American makeup of Family leadership. Each new leadership team needed to include at least one non-American team member. As Hodiah and I were both Americans, we were looking for a new "mate" to join us in the job. Hodiah was as usual quite pregnant, and the travel conditions in the region were pretty rugged. In addition, part of the job description was to encourage, by example, the adoption of the new practices of FFing and its corollary, sharing. (Sharing was the practice of members, married or not, to engage in swapping sexual partners among themselves, in theory to break down walls, encourage unity, and make sure everyone was "getting their needs met.") This pretty well indicated a female was needed for our new teammate. Two guys coming to the door in this context were likely to make a lot of home shepherds a little nervous. Since the area included many countries, often antagonistic to one another, the choice narrowed to a handful of European and Commonwealth single girls. The one who seemed most suited for the position was a very sweet, loyal sister from New Zealand named Sarah, who had been in the Family for less than two years. This little feature of the structural reorganization and the resulting addition of Sarah to our immediate leadership team would dramatically alter the course of each of our lives, and at least seventeen other little ones in its wake.

This period of Family history during the late seventies/early eighties was quite varied from place to place. Some experienced greater freedom to explore personal creative visions with music, media, and even small business ventures. Others were engaged in various internal political purges. Some went just plain nuts, diving into the sexual side of things without reserve. In some areas, the FFing ministry was becoming a euphemism for Escort Service. Marriages were cracking up with the regularity of a demolition derby. Many lives began to unravel, and growing numbers of disciples were drifting, wounded, out of the movement. Through it all, like political tyrants who ride social chaos to power, Mo and Maria continually tightened their grips, weeding out all but the most blindly loyal from the inner circle of leadership.

Our personal history continued to wander further off the map of the known world. Initially our relationship with Sarah was one that developed through our shared sense of mission. Our new coworker was exceptionally personable, diligent, sincere, and teachable. As our friendship with Sarah developed, along with a blending of relationships as she grew close to our kids, we all grew to know and love each other deeply. The mutual relationship grew closer with time, as we experienced the inevitable bonding produced by friction followed by forgiveness. Shared trials, heartbreaks, laughter, and memories multiplied. The practice of sexual sharing resulted in a potent intimacy as well the intense complications that such relationships involve. (See the books of Genesis, and I and II Kings for some historic precedents.) We were still primarily a working relationship at heart, with Hodiah and myself being senior partners and the new team member, Sarah, a junior partner in official matters. Although we were growing closer day by day, Sarah was not as of yet, in a really permanent way, a part of our family. (The idea of "threesomes"—bigamous marriages—was accepted as biblical in the Family, although only very occasionally practiced, and we had not yet committed to this in any formal way.)

As the months and years passed, the lines blurred more and more. Eventually the more or less inevitable happened, and Sarah became pregnant. The father-to-be was a former romantic interest of Sarah's from her life in London prior to joining the group. A successful musician, he'd visited us in India and Greece for extended periods. Sarah had been witnessing to him in the spirit of the times, which led to the pregnancy. When he decided against forsaking his career and lifestyle to become a gospel gypsy, I accepted the emotional and practical role of father to the new baby. This, in turn, led to a deeper commitment on my part to Sarah. This change was to be a source of ongoing pain and confusion for Hodiah, despite her incredible graciousness through it all. I was utterly convinced this was the only right, responsible, and Revolutionary way to proceed.

I was simply unable, and to a degree unwilling, to see things any other way.

The narrative here could easily go off to explore the many and varied episodes in the long running soap opera of our love lives. Although it might provide a plot for a cable TV show, I don't believe it would shed a great deal of light on the essential direction of the journey, or the spiritual implications to which it may point. The complex chemistry of polygamist relationships in the communal context of a group like the Family might even be of some interest from an anthropological or social psychology perspective. What I can guarantee you is that it gave the three of us, and in the years to come our children, an awful lot to chew on. But it really is too much to explore here, other than to say it was another one of those areas springing from the movement's teachings that would make it increasingly complicated for us to disentangle ourselves enough to rethink our directions. Soul ties become so strong and so intertwined that a clear-headed reexamination of our futures became extremely difficult. Alternatives to continuing on the same path become more painful to contemplate. This provided an even stronger unconscious motivation for me to keep my vision tightly focused.

Life, however, has a way of getting in the way of unobstructed views.

CHAPTER 6

HOTEL CALIFORNIA

You can checkout any time you like,
But you can never leave.

~ The Eagles, "Hotel California"

As we traveled throughout the Middle East and India, another plot line was about to intersect with our personal story. Over a year passed in our new responsibilities when I received some disturbing news. Some time before, a close high school friend of mine, Michael, had risen through the ranks to the position of "world servant," which was basically Mo's right-hand man and third highest post in the movement after the king and queen. After years of public praise, Mike had been booted out on charges of disloyalty. This was a pretty devastating blow to me personally, as I had the utmost respect for Mike, and his presence in the inner circle had helped alleviate some of my doubts and fears. His departure left me seriously rattled.

As fate would have it, at this extremely vulnerable stage, I was summoned to the inner sanctum of Mo's headquarters. This was just months after the Jonestown tragedy, and the *International Herald Tribune (IHT)* was beginning a series of stories on some of the world's most high-profile cults. As I boarded the Swissair flight to France, the stewardess offered me a complimentary copy of the *IHT* for in-flight reading. I began to shudder as I realized the front-page story was all about the notorious Moses David and his secret hideout. Beads of sweat began forming on my forehead. I started surreptitiously glancing over both shoulders for signs of anyone tailing me. It wasn't easy to shake a surreal sense of weirdness that was enhancing my already supercharged nervous system as I prepared for I knew not what. Guilt, excitement, fear, hope, and a prayer of "O God, please help me!" swept over me in waves.

As it turned out, I was to share a by-the-week apartment with Mo's daughter Faithy and Peruvian Juan, her mate at that time. They were just returning from a visit with Colonel Mu'ammar Gaddafi in Libya. (Mo had attempted to flatter his way into Gaddafi's good graces, with some temporary success. He seemed to have felt a certain maverick camaraderie with the colonel, and related to his bombastic, anti-Western approach to politics. It all does have a sort of Alice in Wonderland meets Salvador Dali feel to it, doesn't it?)

Our program of activities was to include reading rough drafts of *Mo Letters* and listening to a series of taped personal messages from Maria. We were to respond to these with written reactions that would then be analyzed. There would be visits and interviews with various minions who would size us up, as well as the occasional sharing date with one of Mo's female staff. These dates were designed to strengthen ties but also seemed to serve as strategic information gathering opportunities on behalf of "the Folks," the term used by insiders to refer to Mo and Maria.

Upon arriving in Nice I learned that Faithy and Juan wouldn't be landing until the next day, so Alf, a longtime member of M&M's personal household, was sent to hang out with me until they arrived. Alf was a worker ant type, utterly loyal to all things royal. We had some odd conversations, but there was one exchange I will never forget, which served to further enflame the roiling mess that was my mind at the time. We got on the subject of Jonestown, and Alf blurted out, with an unselfconscious eagerness, "I would have been a great Jonestowner. If Mo says, 'Drink the Kool-Aid,' I drink the Kool-Aid!"

I gulped in stunned disbelief, while trying not to appear completely freaked out. Clearly, I was entering a Brave New World. My insides felt like I had been living on Turkish coffee for a week. Alf had unintentionally introduced me to an inner circle mindset I had never before encountered so bluntly in the Family. That night I lay staring at the ceiling for quite a while. Wowee wow wow.

The next week was one of intense mental and spiritual turmoil. The Folks had a battery of revelations that I was to read and react on. I knew my reactions would be scrutinized for signs of any doubt or disloyalty. The objective, it turned out, was a sort of job interview for a position in the absolute inner circle, as a rotating world service servant. Many of the *Mo Letters* rough drafts had to do with Michael's perceived crimes against the crown, and reacting to these was tearing me asunder, to put it in biblical language. His downfall was clearly stated to have been his carnal mindedness, a false intellectuality, and a misplaced sense of integrity, all born of pride. (Read: a return of common sense.) If I sympathized with Mike it would be obvious that my carnal mindedness, intellectual pride, and misplaced integrity were pulling me towards that same dangerous fate.

Instinctively, I realized only an unequivocal "Amen!" to all, along with a self-flagellating confession of my own weakness along the same lines would pass muster. This we all understood. This route would also serve to erase any remaining vestiges of personhood that might have survived the winnowing thus far. I am ashamed to admit I did, to a large extent, yield to this debasement, though at the time it was all "as unto the Lord."

Even then, some hidden hesitation must have come through. Although I remained under consideration for the position, the impression I made on Mo was pretty shaky. The Folks stopped in to visit us in the apartment the night before I was scheduled to depart for further training at the central administration offices in Switzerland.

At one point Mo locked in on my eyes with an unflinching, searching gaze. He told me that after my training in Switzerland, I was going to return to be with my family in Greece. The plan was not for me to be a full-time member of their staff but rather to be part of a proposed rotating team of three to fill Michael's empty post. Reading my reaction, he clearly was disappointed I was not begging to be allowed to forsake my family and dwell in his tent permanently from that point on.

As he shared this news, my emotions burst and tears streamed down my cheeks in a sudden release of tension. He asked me in an almost pitiful tone at my failure to leap at the brass ring, "Son, are you crying because you are happy or because you are sad?" All I could say was, "I really don't know, sir. Both, I guess." Clearly I was no Alf, and quite possibly I was another sad Michael type of disappointment waiting to happen. An inexplicable feeling of hollowness settled over my soul. And the fate I would meet in a few months was no doubt set in motion in that strained and strange exchange.

Back in Greece, it was early summer. Our family was now a threesome (with one pregnant) and five lovely and lively children. We stayed busy with our shepherding duties and witnessing as well as our customary diversions such as daily walks to the beach with the kids, and our various and sundry trials. Suddenly, in mid July I got a message to be at our downtown office home for a phone call the next day, as we had no phone line at our rustic rural home. I traveled nervously to an office apartment in Athens, still in the dark as to the nature of the call, or even exactly whom it was from.

The caller turned out to be Maria. It seemed that Michael, now back in our hometown in the States, had called World Service (WS) Headquarters in Switzerland trying to reach me with news of my father's sudden and unexpected death. As my family had no way to reach me, Michael had sought contact with me through WS at my family's request. I was counseled to return to the funeral, and also commissioned to give a certain message to Michael from the Folks.

To be suddenly faced with my father's death and be back at home after living in such a completely different world for so long was quite a shock. My father's wake and funeral were deeply trying emotionally. I felt so sad and guilty that I had not seen him in years. He had only briefly met my two oldest kids when they were infants, and now he was gone. I was in shock.

From our little hometown of sixteen thousand, over the years more than a dozen people had followed me into the Family, including both of my brothers. I was by this time the only one still in the group. I had done an excellent job of alienating virtually everyone in my family, as well as our circle of friends. Everyone was quite familiar with many of Mo's wilder theological rants, and clearly thought I was only a few steps from a Jonestown episode.

Mike and Deb, his wife and my dear friend since early grade school, were incredibly gracious to me, understanding my dilemma perhaps better than anyone else on earth. Their Christian spirit and lack of venom even after all the demeaning and untrue things written about them was very confusing. My emotions toward them, the rejection I felt all around, my brokenness over my father's death, and witnessing my mother's grief, all piled on top of my internal efforts to remain uncompromisingly loyal to the Revolution, were a recipe for shattering any solid sense of certainty. I was no longer living from the inside out but trying to figure out the right way to react to the external events that seemed to be coming at me like a Leonid meteor shower. By the time that I had returned to Europe my emotional gyroscope was spinning wildly out of control.

Within weeks of my getting back to Greece, Faithy and Juan visited us. They happened to arrive as we were dealing with a bout of whooping cough that was walloping our children. (Inoculations were strongly discouraged in the Family's theology.) Faithy and Juan were on a mission to set up a recording studio for some Family musicians, including Jeremy Spencer of Fleetwood Mac fame, whom they had recently rescued from pursuing a worldly recording career. But they also were on a mission to scout out the state of the kingdom in

Greece. The fact that my state of mind after returning from the States was somewhat shaken, coupled with some words from Mo about his reservations concerning "poor Kenaz," no doubt had Faithy and Juan already alert for signs of trouble with me. Now the fact that my children were ill was read as a confirming sign of the Lord's displeasure, and they became certain that God was dealing with me. Their powers of discernment went into overdrive.

As autumn approached it became clear that trouble was brewing. I was about to experience the unique privilege of worldwide public berating. Faithy solicited a list of allegations against us from brethren whom we had long counted as dear friends. These charges were not only brought without our knowledge, but we were also given no opportunity to address them from our perspective. They were simply released in print for the whole Family as fact, and with confirming comments from Mo to underline their veracity and spiritual seriousness. This, by the way, came shortly after we had learned that both of the females in our threesome were now pregnant.

As the dark, drizzly days of Athenian winter rolled in, our moods were suited perfectly to the clime. There is nothing like the one-two punch of being vigorously rebuked by God's End Time Prophet and his equally fiery daughter while simultaneously having old friends cross the street to avoid you. There were more than a few evenings when the only way I found to bring an end to the ache was self-medicating with Greece's famous, and dangerously inexpensive, cognac. I took long walks through the hills where I would talk out loud to God, questioning Him about many things, and then cracking open my pocket Bible in hopes I could discern some clear guidance. Needless to say, this is not exactly one of the most highly recommended spiritual disciplines. I was melting down.

By this time I did not really even like Mo anymore. I would have welcomed a green light from God to leave at that point. But I liked myself even less, both for what a failure I was, and for the unconscionable way I was beginning to feel towards God's Anointed. A line from a poem I'd memorized in grade school began to ring in my head: "'Elbow Room!' cried Daniel Boone…" I started to study the world map on our wall and began working on a plan to leave Greece and head back to the wilds of Asia, seeking a distant corner where we might return to a simpler missionary lifestyle. It would also, hopefully, give us a place out of the spotlight to lick our wounds and escape the pressures faced by fallen leaders in more heavily populated centers of Family activity in Europe. We were soon heading back to India and Sri Lanka, and the next epoch in our personal history.

CHAPTER 7

CRACKS IN THE DYKE

If I listened long enough to you
I'd find a way to believe that it's all true,
Knowing that you lied, straight faced, while I cried
Still I look to find a reason to believe.

~ Tim Hardin, "Reason to Believe"

The next decade was a strange mixture of time grinding on and time flying by. From Greece we moved onto India, Sri Lanka, the USA, Mexico, Egypt, Greece again, India again, England, and finally back to the USA. Our missionary activities and efforts to support ourselves during this time ranged from music outreaches with the kids (who achieved some amazing levels of popularity at various times and places), personal and street evangelism, distributing Family literature and media productions, holding Bible studies for the public, radio outreach and follow-up, itinerating at churches, small import-export ventures, and ministering to many friends and contacts from hippies to government ministers. In retrospect, my evaluation of the legitimacy of these evangelistic efforts is mixed. It wasn't all good or all bad. Some efforts had more positive motives and effects than others. Although I have many regrets about these efforts, most of the time we were trying the best we could to follow God's direction and fulfill the Great Commission, as we understood it at that time.

Our family's ranks gradually grew to include seventeen children. (As you may have guessed, the group rejected birth control. My Catholic mom used to ask me with significant puzzlement, "This is the *one* thing you agree with the Pope about?") The story of this population explosion is woven in with the crossing of many oceans, borders, and points of no return. Events tend to blend together in my memory, with chronologies overlapping like the editing of some sort of avant-garde film. My wife and I once tried to make a list of all the homes we'd lived in over the twenty-plus year period of our time in the group. We quickly filled three sheets of paper...and still couldn't account for one whole year. Many details disappear or drift into dreams remembered. There were many moves and migrations, miracles and messes, sometimes all at once! One example of this was how en route to Sri Lanka, due to a visa delay, we found ourselves temporarily homeless in India. A wealthy friend offered us the use of his electricity-free mountaintop meditation retreat in a hill station outside of Bombay. This sounds idyllic, until you consider we had seven children at the time, with two in diapers. Disposables had not yet reached India, and our cloth diapers refused to dry due to the fact it was monsoon season and we were virtually always in a cloud. After tearing up most of our towels and some of our bedding to make do, we finally walked down the mountain and rented a hotel room simply to dry diapers with a hand held hairdryer!

Being real people with complex survival issues and even more complex relationships, many parallel story lines were unfolding in almost Dickensian fashion. But for the purpose of this narrative, I'll stick to how the movement's meanderings continued to affect our own.

The atmosphere in the Family during these years (late 1970s to late 1980s) varied greatly from time to time, depending on the latest directives from "Heaven," and from place to place, depending on the local leadership and organization. As I've mentioned, there were occasional oasis of relative freedom and happiness, but the general trend was towards an ever-tightening centralized control. Shepherding increasingly became fear-based micromanagement. Opportunities for independent action or creativity gradually dwindled to almost nil.

During this period Mo's disastrous sexual teachings and practices veered into the even more catastrophic realm of adult-child sexual contact. There are ample reasons to believe that Mo had molested at least one of his adolescent daughters in the years prior to the launch of the Family. But the way the topic of adolescent sexuality was introduced to the group was through Mo's teaching that in the Bible, as in many cultures throughout history, females were considered marriageable at puberty or shortly thereafter, and that he believed this to be a natural part of God's plan. This eventually led to many heartbreaking outcomes.

In retrospect, this development came to have such horrendous impact on hundreds of children who had been born into the movement during this phase that this much-publicized disaster has come to color everything else about the group. It is a huge topic, and one that I will get to soon. However, in terms of the unfolding of my story, it did not play the central role that it would eventually come to play for the movement as a whole.

But what did influence the course of our personal journey most immediately was the way the issue dramatically altered the public's reaction to the movement. Wacky adults with a strange cocktail of religious spiritualism and aberrant sexual beliefs and practices are one thing. Published photos of adult females engaging in a highly sexualized, disturbing (and criminal!) approach to the child rearing of Maria's son is a completely different matter. It should be noted that many within the movement recoiled from these teachings, and although many stayed, they inwardly determined not to be drawn into these areas. Nonetheless, once this material started hitting the news media, regardless of what practices individual homes may or may not have been engaged in, life anywhere in the movement was dramatically altered by the intense public outcry and the resulting security crises. Even folks who haven't shared mainstream society's sense of the normal/abnormal for many years could not help but notice this topic was extremely volatile, and created all kinds of new risks for everyone involved in the Family.

As of the late 1980s, the children who were victims of this disastrous experiment were mostly still in the group and too young to really process or publicly protest these encounters. But there were a handful of highly publicized legal battles in a few countries, triggered primarily by adult ex-members who were aware of the teachings and practices. Even in areas without these legal situations, the threat of the possible loss of their children created an atmosphere of intense fear and paranoia. Although, as it has been observed, it's not paranoia if they really *are* after you!

In terms of how this atmosphere affected life in the average Family home, the result was felt primarily in two ways. Firstly, outreach and fundraising became increasingly difficult. It came to be seen as high risk to allow outsiders, even those we were evangelizing, to know where we lived or even our phone number. This made it rather difficult to maintain any real sense of missionary zeal. Self-preservation trumped love for the lost. Secondly, it forced the implementation of elaborate security precautions and policies. Due to the high stakes for all, any failure to follow these rules precisely became a serious disciplinary matter. This atmosphere ramped up discipline and control in every area of community life. Authoritarianism swelled to science-fiction proportions. Independent thinking, never a strong suit in the Family, became the mark of someone in serious need of retraining.

None of this was initially obvious to me at the time. My discontent was growing steadily, but was somewhat checked by decades of the habitual self-editing of my thought life. Yet the spiraling ratio of bad fruit to good fruit within the movement, coupled with the rapid proliferation of chokingly oppressive bureaucratic control, finally began to reach a critical mass in my consciousness.

At the time we were living in London. I had begun to take a fresh look as some of the biblical passages that were key ingredients of the fantasy glue that held the Family's theology together. As

I was reading through the Gospels I was struck by the sharp contrast between how the utterly free Jesus who strode through pages of the gospel narrative bore no resemblance to the uptight spirit that was now roaming through the myopic hierarchy of the movement. Reading on in the New Testament, it became clear to me that the flow of authority and leading of the Holy Spirit in the early church recorded in Acts and the Epistles in no way reflected the foul energy moving in our midst. These insights certainly did not make it any easier to click my heels and salute.

At the time, the only way I could explain to myself these painful discrepancies, the oddness of the Family's sexual beliefs and practices, involvement in supposed communication with departed spirits, and the way-beyond-quirky workings of Mo's private world was to credit it all to some "new dispensation" released by God's special Prophet of the End. We viewed David Berg as the "David" prophetically spoken of (according to our beliefs) in Ezekiel 34 and 37, Hosea 3:5, and several other Old Testament passages. This unique basis for authority justified in our minds a departure from traditional Christianity as radical in spirit as the change God's people experienced passing from the Old Covenant to the New Covenant.

During this same period, I began studying our End Time chronology for classes I was giving to the public at a London hotel. In seeking a way to explain our teachings without specifically referencing the *Mo Letters*, I was digging into some parallel passages in the prophets that touched on these David revelations. This study eventually led me to a conclusion that most biblical commentators hold obvious but which hit me with the power of direct revelation: these passages could only be references to the Messiah! Suddenly, the whole basis for those doctrines that had led us away from orthodox Christian theology appeared to be a house of cards built solidly on a foundation of sand. And a storm was just over the horizon.

The process of unraveling the web of self-deception I had to construct to support our erroneous belief system was complex. Like untangling the knots in two one-hundred-foot strings of Christmas lights tossed together last January 2, it involved a lot of sorting out and tracing things back to their beginnings. Beginning to recognize my predicament felt like Gulliver awakening to find that while he slept, the Lilliputians had bound him strand by strand.

The prophet Isaiah illustrated the condition eloquently in chapter 44 of the book bearing his name. He describes a carpenter who selects a piece of wood out of which he carves an idol of his own design. Part of the wood he uses for cooking and heat, while the other part becomes the god of his own making that he incongruously worships. Isaiah speaks of this self-delusion in verse 20: "He feedeth on ashes. A deceived heart hath turned him aside, that he cannot deliver his soul, nor say, 'Is there not a lie in my right hand?'" Bingo!

But now what? The tangles weren't simply doctrinal. Years of relationships, marriage, children, friendships, shared dreams, commitments, and the stuff of life built line upon line completely engulfed me. Even if truth could be easily discerned after years of intensive programming, that discernment would not in itself unravel all the realities that had spread like kudzu vines through the years.

I was heavily invested. Simply walking away at this stage seemed not only impossible, but also irresponsible. My effort to sort out doctrinal truth was complicated by the life-altering implications to which that truth might point. If the Family was wrong, and it was wrong to continue living in its moral framework, then what was the alternative? What would my mates say if they were aware of my doubts? If I opened my heart and spoke out, how would my being sent for retraining and losing what little control that I had benefit my family? Getting kicked out would precipitate a crisis that would have untold consequences for my family. The future to which this path pointed seemed exceedingly bleak. This black hole was beyond my ability to contemplate. Like a harried sheepdog, I scrambled to chase these unsettling thoughts back in another direction.

But how could I continue on if the foundation upon which we'd built all of our dreams was unsound? Would all of our efforts and sacrifices end up as "wood, hay, and stubble?" How could I possibly proceed, business-as-usual, without showing my cards—my growing disillusionment with the Family?

Noted psychiatrist and author M. Scott Peck has compared the process by which we assess and negotiate reality to making "a map with which to navigate the terrain of life." He explains:

> *But if our maps are to be accurate we have to continually revise them... we are daily bombarded with new information as to the nature of reality. If we are to incorporate this information, we must continually revise our maps, and sometimes when enough new information has accumulated we must make very major revisions. The process of making revisions, particularly major revisions, is painful, sometimes excruciatingly painful. And herein lies the major source of the ills of mankind. What happens when one has striven long and hard to develop a working view of the world...and then is confronted with new information suggesting that that view is wrong and the map needs to be largely redrawn?*[24]

It is easy to see this principle at work in normal everyday life and the significant challenges that can result from it. But for a citizen in a totalistic community, especially one in which all of life is supposedly ordered by Almighty God and all personal relationships are built upon this foundation, the challenge is so huge that questioning the map in any fundamental way is generally avoided at all costs.

Still, Jesus describes the Holy Spirit as the Spirit of Truth. Eventually some light can no longer be successfully blocked out. When there is a convergence of intellectual and spiritual insights, coupled with a growing emotional discontent, the distortions on the map start to become clearer and clearer. Despite the fears of what the implications might be, that desire for a truer understanding of what was really going on drew me forward, almost against my own will. Eventually, truth overrode fear.

There is a classic scene in the film *The Matrix* when Neo starts coming unglued from his own reality, as he is drawn toward a deeper level of truth. After a series of tests, he is eventually brought to a place of decision. He can choose the blue pill and be returned to his previous reality with no memory of the challenges to that reality that he has just experienced. If he takes the red pill, he will see the truth and be forever cut off from returning to that previous, somewhat less frightening way of viewing the world. The scene is quite suspenseful and captures well the hesitation we all face at the threshold of costly, even life-shattering discoveries. The "old bottle" stares suspiciously at the "new wine." Coming to grips with the huge distortions in the map we've traveled by for decades can almost feel like Neo being whipped into the behind-the-scenes realities sustaining the illusion of the Matrix. It can feel like dying—and in a way it is.

The process of breaking loose of the grip is gradual, tentative. The mind and heart are simultaneously exhilarated by the hint of freedom as well as held in check by caution. There is that hyper-alert state, like a squirrel nervously measuring each inch towards the picnic table scraps, its desire arm-wrestling with its fear. It edges forward uncertainly like an object caught between two gravitational pulls, seesawing back and forth.

For months I walked a tightrope, trying to avoid preaching things I no longer believed, sticking to the things I still felt were sound. It was not always possible, but I tried to limit my hypocrisy when I could. My wife grew more and more aware of my dissatisfaction, but she thought it was mainly due to my frustration with the nitpicking legalism of our immediate overseers at the time. I was rising early and staying up late studying the Bible, and my conviction that we were wrong on many issues grew continually stronger. I prayed long and hard for grace and guidance.

From the moment that I allowed myself to consciously reexamine our beliefs, with an openness to accept the possibility that we were wrong, that I was wrong, that our lives were being colored and shaped by all this wrong, it was like unleashing a storm in my soul. Life was proceeding all about me. We were witnessing, teaching, counseling, praying, going to leadership meetings, making decisions based on the *Mo Letters*. Yet there was a constant undercurrent, a life beneath the strata of this daily life, an ongoing conversation like the interior dialogue found in the Psalms, searching for God's guidance, seeking His wisdom, mercy, and grace. Through the struggles of daily life I looked for signals, signs, omens, confirmations. My mind worked on the problem, trying to figure things out rationally and scripturally.

"My spirit made diligent search," to borrow the psalmist's phrase. Looking at the problem head-on, with all its frightening ramifications was almost beyond me. So I just went along, one foot in front of another, trying to keep options open, avoiding having to be to definite about things even in my private thoughts, being pulled and tugged in varying directions.

Eventually, due to visa restrictions we were going to have to leave England. I took the opportunity to plan a trip back to the US, where the leadership structure was looser. The States was considered a place for weaker brethren or for temporary missions of re-supply before a change of field. I saw it as a place that would allow for greater freedom of choice and the possibility of creating an alternative future, spiritually and economically.

This move did mean the temporary splitting up of our threesome. Sarah was not a US citizen, which created visa complications, and was pregnant, which raised its own issues. But we'd lived through separations before, and they were not that uncommon in the Family. With plans to reunite when the visa got worked out, we parted. (This situation lasted quite a bit longer than we'd first imagined… but I'll come back to Sarah and the kids' paths again later.)

Shortly after our arrival, the Family in the US began to get organized, and the noose of leadership once again began to tighten about my collar. Simultaneously, there arrived a new series of revelations regarding security, which meant a fresh crackdown and intensifying reign of paranoia, as well as even tighter restrictions and control. It felt like that garbage chute scene in *Star Wars* where the walls start closing in on Han Solo and his colleagues. The pressure was building.

A message slowly began to take shape in my mind, coming together magnetically like metal shavings in an Etch-a-sketch. It started out hazily, like one of those ill-defined weather systems just off Bermuda, but this one was forming somewhere between my subconscious and my lower intestines. It was working its way slowly through my nervous system, eventually setting off a tingle on the skin just above my ears, nibbling ever so tentatively at the edges of my consciousness. Suddenly, it short circuited all kinds of neural pathways, arching across synapses and popping out of my mouth unfiltered, framed by some sort of metaphysical comic strip bubble, and feeling distinctly God-breathed and ever so matter-of-fact: "This is complete bulls__t!" At times it seems even the Holy Spirit may find only the Olde English term appropriate.

Once I'd uttered it, even to myself, I could no longer cram it back in without anyone noticing. By that point I just didn't care anymore. It felt better than letting a particularly urgent but long suppressed burp finally escape. There is a sort of echoing shock to the moment as it rattles around in your skull, as different parts of the brain take stabs at trying to assess the repercussions. The page had been turned. The cat was definitely out of its bag!

Shortly after this realization, during a visit from our area shepherds, I finally erupted. I was clearly chafing at some new dictum that made absolutely no sense, and my body language was screaming when the shepherd confronted me, asking with an air of putting me in my place, what I thought should be done. Needless to say, a sizable chunk hit the fan.

For the next few days my life entered the twilight zone. My wife was in utter shock. The shepherds were stunned by the lengthy list of things I found dangerously unscriptural, counterproductive, foolish, and abusive. Our immediate overseers were fairly inexperienced and fumbled unsuccessfully to try and refute my position. Given my personal history and longstanding reputation, they decided to report the situation to the Folks and get their counsel. The rest of the members of the home immediately began to keep their distance, fearing any possible contagion, as we awaited the verdict from on high.

I was asked to make a tape to be forwarded to them by modem, explaining my feelings. This was an intensely emotional exercise, a dam breaking within me. Out poured Bible verses, historical observations, angry accusations, humble pleas for anyone to answer my questions, and years of pent-up frustration all swirling in a matrix of varied emotions and heaving out of me amid a heavy flow of tears and snot.

I felt empty, too drained to be worried about what was next. At the same time, I felt an immense internal relief and some strange exhilaration at having finally faced the truth, whatever the consequences. It was the only real option. There was an almost eerie feeling; the strange calm before the storm. Uncertain of what would follow, I waited for the other shoe to drop. There I stood. I could do no other.

CHAPTER 8

THE FORK IN THE ROAD

Well I've been afraid of changin'
'cause I've built my life around you
But time makes you bolder
Even children get older
And I'm getting older, too.

~ Fleetwood Mac, "Landslide"

When you come to the fork in the road, take it.

~Yogi Berra

There is an unforgettable scene at the end of the classic sixties film *The Graduate*. The main character, played by Dustin Hoffman, has gone through a complete alienation from the world of his parents and their circle of friends. He has faced the hypocrisy in society as well as the compromise in his own soul, and finally breaks free of all restraint, disrupting the wedding of the girl he loves to the socially acceptable choice of her parents. As they flee the church, they leap on a bus, exhilarated and joyous at having broken the chains of control.

As the bus pulls away, and the huge question of what lies ahead for them starts to sink in, their countenances flatten to a hollow uncertainty. The viewer is left ambivalent as to the emotion of this last scene.

That is the feeling that seemed to hover over my head in the days that followed. My wife Hodiah had been completely taken by surprise in all of this and was having a hard time even framing the issues, much less making a decision about whether to remain a loyal disciple or to stay with her husband. Was there any hope of preserving her family and riding out this mystery storm until her shattered world might come back together somehow? Although the fallout of my tape-recorded "Ninety-five Theses" was still pending, it was clear I would not be continuing on as shepherd, or even as a sheep, in the Family.

From a practical point of view, the rented house in which we were living was in my name. There was the pending sale of a car in my name that was awaiting paperwork, as well as other practical questions. It was decided I should spend a few days with an old friend, an ex-member who lived a couple of hours away, while the various puzzle pieces fell into place. This would give my wife and the shepherds time to think through the issues and receive counsel from the Folks.

Those few days are a blur. They remind me somewhat of the initial shock of grief when learning of the unexpected death of a loved one. Your system overloads. You can't seem to process the information or make any sense of what needs to happen next. What I felt was just a terrible grief, an aching loneliness, and in my case, unbidden tears. The dream that I had watched slowly die over many years, despite occasional rebounds, was finally and irretrievably dead.

Huge questions loomed ahead. What would my wife do? How would my older kids, three of whom were in other parts of the world, react? How would it impact Sarah and our kids in England? What would my family look like in the days and years to come? How would we make it financially, spiritually, emotionally?

For a believer, the natural place to turn when life serves up its larger slices of unexpected crises is to God, but my perception of my access to His throne was wrapped up in my identity as a faithful disciple. What was I now? How did He view me? Had I failed by not persevering somehow? Or had I built my entire life on a lie? Or was there a complicated blending of reality and deception that would take years to sort out? And how was my relationship to God going to be affected by all this? Would my prayers work? What should I be praying for? With thousands of scriptures committed to memory I could come up with answers to these questions fairly easily, but unfortunately I found several different answers to each. On which was I to lean my full weight and trust?

I knew this walk of faith had just taken a dangerous turn into unknown terrain. I wanted to be able to sing with conviction:

We have come this far by faith, leaning on the Lord,
Trusting in His Holy Word, He's never failed me yet.

But my emotions weren't anywhere near calm enough to focus, to make an act of will, a stand of faith. It felt more like I was hanging onto a piece of wood from a capsized boat in a massive storm. After a few days away I received word that I should come back to the home, as counsel had arrived. When I returned, I learned that the Folks had declined to answer any of my questions, and had decided I might be happier in some other place of Christian service. (Does a career of over twenty years of faithful service deserve an answer? Nah.) Before I went back to find out about my wife's decision and take whatever steps that decision led to, I was first asked by the shepherds if I would be willing to sign all my parental rights over to my wife. The idea was to limit whatever harm I might bring upon the work if Hodiah stayed, and I were to end up joining the ranks of that most dreaded of all spiritual forces, "our enemies."

This idea was met with a less than favorable response from me. The biblical expression "exceedingly chafed in their minds, as a bear robbed of her whelps" jumps to mind. Perhaps they saw the word *ENEMY* glowing in red letters on my forehead, I don't know. When they saw that my reaction was volatile, the backpedaling began. Before long they seemed less inclined to urge Hodiah to stay if it might mean this guy with the popped-out blood vessels in his neck might be circling the camp. Hodiah's dismay over leadership's handling of this matter, as well as their decision that I should sleep in my car in a supermarket parking lot that night, may have added weight to the teetering scales of her decision.

Thankfully, she decided to follow her poor benighted husband into "the pit." This was the result of her inability to watch the dissolution of our family of twenty years, as well as her hope that eventually I would return to my senses and rejoin God's End Time Army. Whatever her reasoning, for this I give abundant thanks to the God of heaven.

After another troubled night outside of Winn-Dixie, I returned to finish loading up for our departure. Thankfully, we had a van and a tiny travel trailer from which to launch our new life. The shepherds took one more run at getting me to sign over my fifteen-year-old daughter. "Ree-jected!" as NBA announcer Marv Albert might put it. We finally set off, a dejected, fractured group slinking rather hopelessly toward an unknown future. No "Hallelujah Chorus" filled the air as the brave pioneers ventured forth. The statement "things could be worse" would have been greeted as being wildly optimistic. We were just another family of poor white trash with a Bible on the dashboard, crawling down the highway to Flip-flop City, Florida.

We were kindly received by a former colleague from our days in India and the Mid East, the ex-member who had put me up for those few days of waiting. Roland was now the single parent of seven kids, his wonderfully loving wife, Carol, having tragically died of breast cancer a few years previous. The story of his separation from the group was a monument to cult insensitivity. Carol's passing at the end of a lengthy and painful illness happened to coincide with some push to tighten up, meant to weed the ranks of the less loyal and (always suspect) independent types. Roland was very practical, and he had wisely bought a small fixer-upper farmhouse for the price of what he would have flushed down the rent hole in a year or so. He had a few Family folks staying with him at the time of Carol's death. Within days of the burial, these brethren had all been advised by long-distance phone calls from leadership that if they wanted to keep their membership status, they would need to move to homes on the East Coast in order to meet some arbitrary new fellowship requirements. Roland found out about it all, and his limited options, by a phone message on the answering machine after the others were already quietly making departure plans. Father and children were more than a little spiritually bruised by this incredible lack of kindness.

Given these experiences, Roland was not inclined to judge us for leaving the fold. That alone was a huge comfort. His kids were also a great blessing to our family. We shared many offspring of overlapping ages, so some socialization and playmates were in place. We all grew very close to this family and continue to this day to share a bond that only something like this set of circumstances can create.

Little miracles of mercy went before us as we found an affordable little cinder block home on a couple of acres just around the corner from our refugee encampment in Roland's yard. Life was a struggle and creature comforts were few. Income initially came from a variety of channels, ranging from food stamps and odd jobs such as picking tomatoes and cleaning supermarket floors to occasional singing gigs with the kids. We became involved in a small start-up mission church that, although a little dysfunctional, was nonetheless very loving and accepting towards us. They even had me teaching some Bible classes, and my wife (now returning to her legal name, Stephanie) helping with children's outreach and Vacation Bible School. These little things really did help ease the pain a bit. At least they put off cold turkey withdrawals from a sense of being "in ministry."

This transition period lasted over three years, with some intervals of traveling, usually in an old motor home. I got to see many of America's most wonderful sights from the underside of a twenty-six-foot 1976 Southwind. There is nothing like crossing Arizona in the summer with a shaky air-conditioner. Ah, the sight of the purple mountains majesty and hearing the death rattle of your air-con while your adolescent kids are wondering about what the heck their evil, sadistic parents were thinking. I wish I could report a smooth transition from mindless cult-zombies to well-adjusted all-American family. Alas, this was not the case. We were a floating catastrophe. None of us had any idea how to proceed from point A to point B. My wife was, for several years, still mentally in the Family, blaming our many and sundry battles on my backsliding. My kids were on a slow boil in a pot of psychological goulash, seasoned with adolescent hormones and culture shock.

I was a depressed and moody mass of confusion and frustration, without a clue of how to raise kids in this society, which seems to be quite a challenge to even the best qualified. Memories of myself during this period bring a bright redness to my cheeks, as images of mentally unstable hillbilly preachers standing against the onslaught of the Great Whore Babylon come to mind. I was an ayatollah in flip-flops. After one of my devotional rants, my most piercingly honest daughter commented to her mother: "I understand what Dad says about Mo not being God's End Time Prophet, but sometimes I think he must think *he is*!" Ouch. She had a point there, though Mom had the sense not to mention it to me until quite a bit later.

Eventually we managed to make a little financial headway, with gradual improvements in living conditions. Although neither I nor my wife would be described as being mellow, we did begin to bring the emotional shooting war into somewhat of a détente. Then some dear friends of ours from India and the Mid East called us with the excellent news that they, too, had been offered the left foot of fellowship and were working with a few other Family outcasts in New England. We had some business opportunities in that general area planned for the summer, so we began planning a visit.

Within a few months we sputtered up North in our old motor home. We had planned on spending a few days feeling things out, and then a few weeks praying and thinking over possibly relocating to the general vicinity for some like-minded fellowship. We were very lonely and really not connecting spiritually with any of the churches we'd tried. Within hours of our arrival, one of the brothers there came up to us with a classified ad of a house for rent just a few miles away. To make a long story short, within a few days of arriving in New England we had rented a lovely (needs TLC) rural home on thirty wooded acres, complete with its own bass pond.

Within a few more weeks we were part of a bustling community of ex-member families, complete with home school co-op, home church, and children's singing group. We had close to forty offspring among four families, as well as a variety of half-thought-through unresolved issues and hangovers from the Family. Hectic and half-breed though it was, it was still immensely less lonely and more comforting, than the "three-and-a-half years of Great Tribulation" we'd just lived through down in Florida. Many battles remained to be fought and issues wrestled alligator-style towards some resolution. But at least we were among good friends.

All of our lives lurched forward in fits and starts. Business, jobs, teenagers (need I say more?) We shared lots of laughter amid the tears. Denial was doing battle with depression. We shared victories with our fellow victims. There were gigantic Six Flags–size mood swings from hopes for renewed ministry to just keeping our fingers crossed that the kids could stay out of prison. As time passed, at least the most serious delusions seem to shrink and fade like tumors responding to radiation. Life's battles started to resemble those of people in society around us more than the intergalactic adventures of Starship Family. A little boring can be good.

One of the interesting things that was brought into play among our small circle of friends was a referral one couple received when seeking some marriage counseling. Marriages established in the Family carry with them some unusual baggage, to put it mildly. Arranged marriage, sexual sharing, FFing, and bigamy are not all that common, it turns out, in modern America. Have you ever seen a psychologist's eyes glaze over while listening to your story, as he slips into various stages of shock? But this contact was to eventually lead us into a badly needed green pasture beside still waters, where our souls might experience a little further healing.

Our friends had been referred to a counseling ministry with the ponderous name The New England Institute of Religious Research (NEIRR), headed by a former Congregational pastor and his counselor colleague. Our friends raved about the exceptional understanding these folks had for the cult experience. People generally tend to see things pretty black-and-white when it comes to cults. Actually, black-and-black might be a little more accurate. The attitude can be summed up with the slightly altered title "When Bad Things Happen to Bad People." However, these folks had a much different view, valuing the idealism, commitment, and self-sacrifice that motivate many to join these movements. Through wide personal experience and much scholarly research, they had gained a thorough understanding of the psychological and spiritual dynamics inside high-control groups, particularly communal groups.

After we overcame various levels of our own distrust and/or uncertainty, these folks became an incredible resource for gaining the knowledge we needed to understand and to deal with our past. They also found themselves a court of last resort when we would hit various stone walls in the road to recovery, and the struggles of playing catch-up football with life while raising large families.

Picture going through midlife crisis with kids in diapers and kids having kids simultaneously, having the income of a recent high-school grad, while going through major spiritual crises, while married to someone who you thought you knew but is all of a sudden becoming someone else, and you aren't sure you even like the new one. Heck, you were barely adjusting to the old one. Please pass the Prozac.

Our interaction with the NEIRR marked a major turning point in our journey. We now had someone who understood our experience, could help us understand it, and was willing to expend the massive amount of time and energy necessary to help us come to terms with past, present, and future. More importantly, they were deeply spiritual and were solidly grounded in a biblical perspective without some of the unfortunate judgmentalism that can often accompany that package. We took full advantage.

SOMETHING SOMEBODY STOLE

THE FORK IN THE ROAD

CHAPTER 9

ZOMBIES AND SERPENTS

*"Thinking again?" the Duchess asked with another dig of
her sharp little chin.
"I've a right to think," said Alice sharply, for she was
beginning to feel a little worried.
"Just about as much right," said the Duchess, "as pigs have to fly..."*

~ Lewis Carroll, *Alice in Wonderland*

I remember the first time someone recommended that I read a book entitled *Combating Cult Mind Control* by Steve Hassan. I had been out of the group for several years and had already shed many destructive beliefs and much of the controlling conditioning. Nevertheless, that phrase "cult mind control" sent the hackles on the back of my neck into a nervous jig. Mind control? Pictures of a column of bug-eyed zombies, arms outstretched before them, marching slowly forward at the behest of some Svengali popped into my mind. Sheesh. Give me a break. Yeah, I had done some stupid stuff, and swallowed more than my fair share of holy hokum, but I had since encountered numerous churchgoers who appeared almost as gullible. Sure, our doctrine had had a little more *National Enquirer* appeal than most, but our daily existence had become fairly pedestrian. Our lives required a lot of careful planning and thoughtful decision making, as well as a generous sprinkle of flying by the seat of our pants. Our general worldview had many large overlaps with various segments of mainstream society. I did not see myself as having been stumbling through life in a trance and was a little offended by the suggestion. The term itself seemed to drip with the reactionary hyperbole I'd wearied of hearing from angry ex-members who seemed to blame the cult for everything from hopelessness to hair loss. I decided at the time to give the book a miss, not for a moment suspecting that "cult mind control" might actually be triggering my negative reaction.

It was several years later that we were finally introduced to the ex-cult counseling ministry I mentioned led by a gentleman with the unlikely name of Reverend Bob Pardon. Despite our ingrained suspicions, when we finally met Bob and Judy (his colleague and wife) we were greatly relieved to sense in them a gentle, affirming, pastoral concern. They also displayed a greater sensitivity to the spiritual dynamics of the cult experience than we'd ever before encountered in people who hadn't actually been there and done that.

Over time they shared with us the insights and resources that helped us understand the psychological framework of our experience. They took the zombie image out of the issue. They educated us about practical constants that are present in almost any high-control group, regardless of the extreme variations in credo. They helped us discern the pattern of manipulation inherent in all. The curtain was pulled back on the Wizard of Oz's control room and revealed a somewhat pathetic figure, working feverishly away at the controls to produce the illusion. When meeting with former members of widely diverse groups, it was uncanny how many elements of our experiences overlapped. We always got a chuckle over the toilet paper guidelines… was it three sheets of two-ply or two sheets three-ply? It seems cults have a certain business model, regardless of belief system. The menu at McDonalds is different from Taco Bell, but the standard operating procedures are pretty much the same.

The thought reform piece of the puzzle doesn't answer every issue faced by former members, nor do I believe it provides a handy "get-out-of-jail-free" card, absolving all guilt for actions taken while in. But it does provide a very helpful paradigm through which one can approach the task of making sense of one's experience. In his book *Recovering from Churches That Abuse*, Ronald Enroth explains: "They need to understand how the control mechanisms that were at work...continue to affect them after they have left. They need to understand what has happened to them emotionally and psychologically."[5] It does help to see that your behavior was not the result of a rare mental illness or evidence of an unusually weak mind coupled with the backbone of an earthworm. It allows ex-members to find some solid footing as they go on with life. It is a helpful salve to one's self-esteem, which at this stage is decidedly in the negative numbers.

So just what is this "thought reform" business? If one reads through almost any of the books related to high-control groups, it is not long before you stumble onto a list, or group of lists, that deal with the ingredients of the thought reform pie: "2 Elements", "4 Basic Components", "6 Conditions", "8 Psychological Themes" (... and I guess, "a partridge in a pear tree.") This list will vary a little when authors frame the issue in terms of "spiritual abuse" with a little more religious flavoring, but with a lot of overlap as well.

The psychological model that was presented to us seems to be one of the clearest to grasp. This construct was the work of Steve Hassan, a psychologist and veteran of the Moonies. It appears in both of his books, *Combating Cult Mind Control* and *Releasing the Bonds*. It is commonly referred to by its acronym, the BITE Model, which stands for:

I. Behavior Control
II. Information Control
III. Thought Control
IV. Emotional Control[6]

It is well worth getting a hold of Hassan's books and studying this model for yourself. For the sake of this narrative, I will try to briefly summarize the concepts here, with reference to our own experiences with the Family.

I. Behavior Control

This component begins with the regulation of an individual's physical reality. In the Family, as in many other groups, this was accomplished by the call to "drop out of the system" and live communally with other sold-out disciples. Contact with one's biological family and old friends is severely limited. Often, a significant geographic change in the early stages of the process was involved.

Almost everything in a new disciple's environment changes dramatically. In the Family, we "forsook" most of our wardrobes, and these were replaced by clothing of a different style. (The word "style" here applies in the loosest sense!) Changes in hairstyle, diet, and sleep patterns, as well as lack of almost any personal downtime, all begin to redefine one's sense of reality.

Financially, one loses all independence and becomes utterly dependant on the common pot. The control of the common pot is, of course, tightly in the hands of leadership. I can recall how almost four months after joining, the thought struck me that I had not even touched money in that entire time.

As I described in the account of life at the Ranch in Texas, during the earliest stages of the process there is an almost complete lack of self-determination in any aspect of life. Schedules are closely followed. Rules are strictly enforced. Permission is required for almost anything. All of these procedures are justified on the grounds of sacrificing ourselves for the good of the whole. We were training our spirits to walk in humility and obedience before God, and in security and health concerns unique to countercultural communal groups. We were engaged in a great endeavor, fighting a spiritual war of eternal consequence while living behind enemy lines. We ought not even think of indulging our own whims and fancies when so much was at stake! This was a radical reversal of the prevailing motto of our generation, "Do your own thing." That concept was viewed as rank heresy, the voice of Satan himself.

Hassan refers here also to the "need to report thoughts, feelings, and activities to supervisors." The Family developed a daily self-reporting system called the Open Heart Report (OHR). In addition to an account of general activities and progress in scripture memorization progress, it also required a strict critique of one's thought life, with an emphasis on uncovering any hints of doubts or critical thoughts that might have bothered you during that day. It soon became apparent that some degree of self-disclosure was necessary here, especially if you'd seemed to noticeably bristle at any instruction or had been visibly bummed-out by anything. Naturally, all of this information would come in very handy for leadership as they helped you "keep every thought under subjection to Christ"— and to His helpers on earth, of course.

II. <u>Information Control</u>

You may recall the wilderness experience I described at the Ranch. This involved separating us from contact with outsiders except under tightly controlled circumstances and the limiting of all informational sources of input. These were restricted to the Bible, as interpreted and explained in terms of the Revolution, and to a few other carefully chosen and critiqued sources in line with the group's beliefs. Information concerning the inner workings of the movement was heavily filtered on a need-to-know basis and correlated with leadership seniority. Eventually, getting to be in the know became one of the leadership perks that people would strive for, not unlike many less exotic organizational structures in society at large, only cranked up a few notches. Even things such as the evening news broadcasts were to be consumed only with an accompanying commentary to help us see things "God's way."

Once community life had evolved into a routine pattern of outreach, Family literature and media production sales, tightly scheduled childcare and home maintenance, there was a growing vacuum for some form of communal relaxation in the evenings. As video clubs proliferated around the globe and homes began to avail themselves of this entertainment pleasure, Family leadership was quick to act in developing a ratings system. It was quirky to the point of bizarre. Mo would often get some sort of revelation for a film such as *Fire-Starter*, which fed into his conspiratorial and supernatural worldview. These films he would then rate "excellent," despite violent and disturbing content. At the same time, he would be quick to catch the irreparable damage that could be done to a child's mind by a film such as *Chitty-Chitty Bang-Bang*, which was banned for its supposed sympathy towards witchcraft. If a film had any whiff of anti-cult attitude such as *Mosquito Coast*, or *Apocalypse Now*, well, you may as well just go sell your soul to Satan right now rather than watch one of these.

The limiting of information input from the culture at large doesn't leave the disciple with endless hours of unprogrammed mental bandwidth. What we lacked in "system" media was replaced by an endless stream of our own productions. Even the Bible left unfiltered could lead to serious problems, as I can testify. We had hours of live teaching, followed by plenty of recorded teaching. We were acutely aware that music had a huge influence, and listening to "system" music was verboten. The Family worked hard to produce a large quantity of its own music to take up the slack. Eventually these tapes came to be viewed as so important for people's thought lives that before even any Family produced song could be released it was subjected to a careful screening of lyrics and even musical arrangement. Drums and lead guitars both had to be watched carefully for seditious tendencies. So much for "ze revolution."

Under this heading, Hassan also includes "spying on other members" and the "unethical use of confessions." The spying deal began with the buddy system but eventually evolved in a Stalinesque culture of "lovingly" reporting on any of our brothers or sisters who seemed to be starting to color a little too far outside the lines. This, of course, was done with their spiritual best interests at heart. Although being motivated by brownie points would not have been admitted, it was interesting how the most "honest" reporters did seem to rate the uppermost seats at feasts, by some odd coincidence. Think *Animal Farm*, *1984*, *Brave New World*, and *Fahrenheit 451*.

Gut-wrenching confessions also became a normative practice throughout the Family. Not only those with independent streaks, but eventually almost all the top echelon of leaders went through extensive and widely published book-length confessions. This not only succeeded in smashing the egos of all but the Folks, but also provided ammunition that could be held against you should you ever wander off the reservation. When one prominent pioneer left the movement and went public to expose numerous crimes within the Family, he was lambasted on national television with the contents of his coerced confessions. This sensitive soul ended up committing suicide while in a state of deep depression! Perhaps some "confession is good for the soul" as the axiom goes, but in high-control movements, you may want to read the fine print on the warning label very carefully.

III. <u>Thought Control</u>

This section gets at the nub of how high-control groups manage to maintain the loyalty of so many otherwise coherent individuals, in the midst of what appears to outsiders as an utterly nonsensical worldview. During the earliest stages of the thought reform process, the strategies of environmental control and information control must be carefully managed. As the ball gets rolling and the process begins to take root, it eventually becomes self-enforcing. Once a person becomes committed to the vision "as unto the Lord" has gotten the gist of what the goal is for a truly radical disciple, and the new world map is firmly in one's consciousness, the customer himself begins to enthusiastically join in the sales process. Forget the exhortation of a personal trainer, you are going for the burn on your own now, and aren't going to stop until you've got those six-pack abs—or in this case a "yielded and submissive spirit."

The world has been redefined. Like the Ministry of Truth in 1984, the map's lines and alliances have all been redrawn. Black and white. Good and evil. Us and them. Easy peasy.

Along the way, learning to speak a new language helps immensely. Hassan calls this "loaded language." Analytical thinking has been renamed "critical spirit." Freedom of conscience is now "carnal mindedness." Having a different opinion is "rebellion and the sin of witchcraft." Explaining your perspective on an incident has become "self-justification." Thoughtfully processing a new policy is now "pride and self-will." Considering the needs of your wife and kids is now obviously "selfishness and dissembling."

Before long you begin to recognize these "dangerous" tendencies as soon as they start to wheedle their way into your mind. You have memorized verses for just such occasions: "Casting down imaginations and every high thing that exalts itself against the knowledge of God, and bringing into captivity every thought to the obedience of Christ." "Give no place to the Devil."[7] And some helpful Family proverbs such as "You can't stop the birds from flying overhead, but you can keep them from making a nest in your hair." And the all-time favorite:

If you think, think, think,
Your gonna sink, sink, sink,
Because you stink, stink, stink.

You are prepared. You've got on the whole armor of God, the helmet of salvation, the breastplate of righteousness, and the sword of the spirit. Just let that stinkin' devil try something. Rambo is ready!

God forbid if somehow or another one of Satan's sneak attacks gets through and you begin to notice inconsistencies in Family teachings, or a scripture rattles around in your head that casts doubt on some new revelations. Well, then, maybe it's time to go pray in tongues for an hour or so. That will usually do the trick. That will blow out the cobwebs. After that go read a Mo Letter on the danger of doubts, and kill that damn spider!

Brainwashing? Sure! We all need it! Can I lend you a bar of soap?

IV. <u>Emotional Control</u>

Just saying that phrase, lo, these many years hence, is enough to elicit a heartfelt "ouch" from my soul. The manipulation of one's feelings through guilt trips, fears of many species, public humiliation, and ostracizations were elevated to an art form.

Are you or your child sick? Obviously your fault. Is Mo or Maria sick? Your fault. Child wetting the bed? Evil spirits and talismans. Worried about the negative fallout of a decision made while following policy? An attack of the devil. Having doubts about leadership?

You should not have watched the video on the no-watch list, or it might be the result of evil spirits from your ancestors, reading *Huckleberry Finn*, refusing to yield to your leader's lesbian advance, or a stash of white sugar in your pantry. Thinking about breaking a rule, like maybe listening to "system music" or having a third cup of coffee or reading a letter from an old friend who has left the group? Get ready for the boogeyman to get you! Wondering what life would be like if you ever decided to leave? Prepare to spend years in prison on IRS violations or pick a nice spot in a potter's field for after you go crazy and pull a Judas jump.

If you have even dipped your toes in these shark-infested waters of woe, you'd better come clean right now! "Be sure your sin will find you out." Confess, and the Inquisition shall have mercy upon thee. And won't you be as grateful as a puppy once you've gotten it all off your chest and we've allowed you to stay in the Family. Never mind that you are now separated from your wife and kids and doing dishes in Siberia for the next year. It could have been worse. God might have started in on your kids again. Well, yes, of course the Family does have a few small problems now and again, but yours is not to reason why, yours is but to do or die. Even if you obey an order that is wrong, God will bless it.

The real coup de grace comes when one moves from being on the receiving end of these processes to being a willing participant in helping others to "grow" through such ministrations. This becomes massively reinforcing in two ways: 1) as you witness the "great strides" people make as you assist them through these difficult steps; and 2) if you should start to have misgivings along the way, the thought that you were an assisting surgeon in the spiritual lobotomy that dramatically altered the lives of others is enough to make you run back to the "safe thought" zone with a shudder. It just couldn't be wrong. It couldn't. It just couldn't...

After Bob and Judy shared the BITE model with us, we followed it through like a checklist, correlating each point with our experience. We had very few points that didn't rate a large bold X, often highlighted and underlined. It was also really fascinating to see what a tight fit it was with other groups. That was a real eye popper. This insight helped remove some of the mystery, and it was remarkably liberating to see how generic the process really is. The truth, they say, shall set you free.

There were other resources that were helpful in examining our past. We watched a number of videos that looked at some of the group dynamics of social psychology. One in particular was a recording of an episode of *Dateline* that dealt with several fascinating experiments. The first was a black-and-white clip filmed in the fifties of the highly publicized experiment undertaken by Stanley Milgram. In the exercise, two individuals arrive simultaneously at a testing center. An instructor equipped with an official-looking white lab coat and clipboard ushers the two into a room, when one is strapped into a chair and an electrode is connected to his arm. The other individual, who was told he was to act as the teacher, was taken to an adjoining room where he was instructed to read a list of two word pairs. He would then ask the learner to repeat them back. If the learner answered correctly, he would then move on to the next set of words in the series. If the answer was wrong, the teacher was told to administer a shock to the learner. According to the dial, these shocks began at 15 volts and went up to 450 volts in 15-volt increments. The teacher was never coerced into doing so, but simply reminded by the official looking instructor that the experiment required him to continue. In reality, the learner was actually in on the experiment, and no real shock was being administered. What was amazing was that two-thirds of the participants, ordinary people from working, management, and professional classes, fell into the category of obedient subjects. A full 65 percent of all the teachers punished the learners to the maximum of 450 volts, despite the victim's protests and feigned cries of pain! Today this experiment would be deemed unethical due to the high level of stress it caused in its subjects. This and other similar studies reveal our strong desire to conform, certainly calling into question just how independent-minded most people really are.

In addition to looking at these psychological factors, it was also important for us to make sense of the spiritual dimension of our experience in the Family. Christian commentators tend to refer to the phenomenon in terms of spiritual abuse. Here again we encounter the unavoidable lists: 21 Beliefs, 10 Characteristics, 5 Roles and 10 Rules, 7 Dynamics, etc. Again, there is much overlap, but the main thing that this area adds to the discussion is that it focuses directly on issues of faith. David Johnson and Jeff Van Vonderen in their widely quoted and very helpful *The Subtle Power of Spiritual Abuse* broadly define the term as follows:

Spiritual abuse is the mistreatment of a person in need of help, support, or greater spiritual empowerment, with the result of weakening, undermining, or decreasing that person's spiritual empowerment.[8]

This definition may suit many churches and pastors with control issues, but the Family and other totalistic communal groups take it a heck of a lot further than that. Since much of what is written on the subject tends to refer to less extreme fellowships, it is often necessary to crank up the volume on what is being said in order to apply it to more radical expressions of control. What is helpful about this literature is that it ties the damage to the core of a person's spiritual makeup and most basic beliefs about life. (Enter the "serpent" aspect of the "zombies and serpents.") This points to some of the thorniest problems in the recovery process. The good news is there *is* a doctor in the house. The bad news is that *he* is the one who is being carried out on a stretcher!

Awakening from the cult experience, one's interior "Holy of Holies," that sacred place created inside of us for the presence of the Creator alone, feels like a frat house the morning after the toga party. Violations and abominations abound. Surveying the damage, it is not at all surprising that at this stage many are tempted simply to tack a Condemned sign on the property, rope it off for demolition, and walk away, determining to find a route through life that avoids this neighborhood completely.

Even if you decide to work on cleaning the mess up, it can be a daunting task. Survivors of intense spiritual abuse often refer to their experience as "spiritual rape." Many contemporary speakers point out that at its core, the Christian life is not religion but relationship. Healthy relationships are built on trust. Trust is a huge problem for rape victims. When mature believers confront the deepest challenges in life, they lean heavily on the foundation of their conviction of the complete goodness of the God in whom they have placed their trust. What if the concrete of that foundation has been adulterated with clay and the nature of God has been distorted beyond recognition, and then these frauds of monumental proportions are uncovered? If you have just been chomped on by a wolf in sheep's clothing, will you be likely to throw open the door to the next sheep you see through the peephole?

The challenge of how to restore the heart to a place of trust is something I'll visit again later. Understanding just how the serpent sneaked in there to begin with is at least a start. Paul speaks of "not being ignorant of his devices." This knowledge itself unmasks the serpent and breaks the enchantment.

There is a memorable passage in one of C.S. Lewis's Chronicles of Narnia, *The Silver Chair*. The Prince had been captured by a witch, placed under a spell, and taken underground. Most of the time, he was free to roam about, as under the spell he was convinced that the witch was good. He was satisfied to be her slave, with no sense of his own worth. But for one hour each day he would awake from the spell and be fully aware of his true situation. Unfortunately, during these periods of lucidity he was chained to a silver chair and unable to escape. Finally he is set free from his chair and the spell. With his sanity restored he recognizes his rescuers as Narnians. He thanks them for their loyalty to the throne and learns he has been under the spell for ten long years. The prince exclaims:

"Ten years!" said the Prince, drawing his hand across his face to rub away the past. "Yes, I believe you. For now that I am myself I can remember that enchanted life, though while I was enchanted I could not remember my true self."[9]

But remember we must.

CHAPTER 10

O, BROTHER, WHO ART THOU?

What hurts the soul? To live without tasting the water of its own essence.

~ Rumi

I yam what I yam.

~ Popeye

One of the most destructive ends of spiritual abuse is the systematic erasure of the essential core of one's being. There are so many things inherent in our personalities that are unique to us, tied in some way to our identity like our fingerprints or DNA, that "us-ness" that makes us, well, us.

There are, of course, many qualities that we all share in common with the rest of humanity. Paul speaks of the "spirit of man" by which we "know the things of man," but the incredible variety that abounds throughout creation is also reflected in the human family. Having been created in God's image, we seem to reflect something of His "interesting-ness" in the rainbow of personalities we meet around us. Oddly, it appears that there is something about much of religion in general and about cultic religion in particular that seems hell-bent on reducing that explosion of diversity into an assembly line of homogenized, cookie-cutter, "new creatures in Christ." For all the lip service that the Family paid to the noble nonconformists of the Bible—Noah, Moses, Samson, David, Jeremiah, Ezekiel, and their ilk—in reality, the goal was a one-size-fits-all approach. One Mo Letter actually verbalized it, stating the goal of the program was to "raise up an army of little Davids." Another letter noted as praiseworthy the faithfulness of one whose personality resembled a robot. Heck, we even wrote a song about it! Individualism was decried with Maoist zeal. One could imagine it being raised to the level of one of the Seven Deadly Sins. Conveniently, we had already bounced "Lust" off the list, which freed up a spot.

Our journey through the Family took many twists and turns, through different fads and fazes, and the occasional weird little cult-within-a-cult scenarios. One feature that was virtually constant throughout was the never-ending cycle of "breaking and remaking." This was theoretically based on the biblical concept of the Potter and the clay referred to in the prophets and seen in God's dealings with many of His servants in the scriptures. Far from the divinely guided process of the biblical biographies, our experience more closely resembled the spiritual equivalent of Dr. Frankenstein's laboratory. At times we seemed to view ourselves as wizened, supernaturally guided analysts uncovering secrets in peoples' Open Heart Reports, flexing our discernment and prescribing soul-tampering solutions like so many sugar pills from a toy doctor's kit. With a little soundtrack from *Fantasia* thrown in, it would be very close to the Mickey Mouse segment as "The Sorcerer's Apprentice."

Almost anyone who made it through the mid-eighties in the Family has to have vivid, cold-sweat-inducing memories of lengthy *Mo Letters* reading lists and "walkie-talkies." (This referred euphemistically to the systematic deconstruction of the psyche while on a walk with your shepherd. The practice not only kept the wayward in line, but also enabled the shepherd to cross the daily exercise

O, BROTHER, WHO ART THOU?

requirement off his or her to-do list). Some may remember hours and hours of writing "reactions." It may, in fact, cause one to break out in a reaction! This ritual of committing self-criticism to paper reduced the measure of one's spiritual growth to the ability to root out from one's own heart any surviving shreds of individuality or freedom of thought and denounce it with an air of disgust usually reserved for describing the mysterious mold growing on some long-forgotten leftover discovered in a hidden corner of the fridge. We were determined to militantly renounce all such proletarian tendencies with the fervor of Fidel on meth!

This doesn't seem to be the type of spirituality likely to engender a sense of the tender love of the Father for His children. It was more likely to produce the self-loathing you feel when you discover that the unpleasant odor in the room is coming from the sole of your own shoe. Not only does this mindset tend to crush all sense of joy, but it leads to a habit of hunting down your own sins so intently that your whole interior life becomes a meditation on warped motives, finding sinful pride lurking behind every thought and emotion. As one author has put it: "Even when I feel good, I feel bad that I feel good."

Even when by a true miracle of the Spirit of Truth we have been guided out from underneath this malevolent cloud, it can take quite a while before our thoughts begin to escape this dark, free-spinning hamster wheel. What a pleasure to discover that not every Godward thought or prayer needs to be prefaced with a series of mea culpas. Like a dog emerging from a stagnant pond, we feel a need to vigorously shake off the clinging wetness.

Digging out from under the rubble that has entombed our God-given personality can be a painstaking process. Even after we begin to get free, we feel again like timid teenagers. We are sure that everyone is staring at the pimple on our nose, laughing at our white socks with black shoes, and fear that perhaps a "kick me" sign has been scotch-taped to the back of our shirt. Our personalities now seem oddly uneven. In certain areas of experience we may have uncommon breadth and depth. Traveling the world on the cheap while

SOMETHING SOMEBODY STOLE

memorizing thousands of scripture passages and raising a passel of kids in a communal environment is bound to teach you something. Yet in other areas we feel completely green. The normal maturation process one might experience between the ages of twenty and forty years has been derailed and is now trying to find its way back on track. Part of us is still struggling through the transition to the independence of adulthood, while at the same time we are also going through midlife crisis. What fun.

It would be great if we could ease back into life with a year or so of gradual transitioning, like those guys in novels who awaken from a coma after twenty years, with the help of a guide to bring us up to speed. By the way, while you're at it, could you please top up my IRA, sock about ten years of equity in the house, and advance my career to at least middle management? Alas, no such program for reorientation exists. In reality we are faced with needing to change the tire while driving the car.

As you begin to survey the pieces of your fractured sense of identity scattered like so many bits of Humpty Dumpty at the foot of the wall, a sense of anger can start to form out of the pain of the scrambled sight. You feel like ripping away at the constraints that have bound you for years. There is a vague resemblance to the intensity you feel in the teen years, struggling to emerge into a person in your own right, but the lack of the accompanying hormonal surges makes it difficult to sustain quite that level of angst. Sheer fatigue brings on a certain mellowing that might be expected of someone with my hairline and waistline, which at this stage are steadily moving in opposite directions. But doggone it, it does still eat at you, and you do need to do something to try to regroup and get on with things. Sorting through the questions of who we really are and our position in the grand scheme of things seems to be a fairly logical step in preparing the ground for new construction.

To me, this is one of the most exciting bits about beginning a fresh chapter in the journey. Yeah, I know. Your friends still in the movement may view you as something between a "weak sister"

O, BROTHER, WHO ART THOU?

and "God's vomit"—see the message to Laodicea in the Book of Revelation. Your original family and friends seem to be barely able to suppress the screaming "I told you so!" coursing through their neural pathways. Your own kids seem to be staring at the large red L (for loser) tattooed in the middle of your forehead. The pastor to whom you have gone for advice is trying to discern exactly how many demons you have and what their names are while browsing through his day planner for a convenient time to schedule an exorcism. I won't even get into what the good folks at the food stamp office are thinking about your family planning choices. It does seem obvious that looking for self-definition in the eyes of others may not be the best route forward.

So it's back to the ol' "who am I?" Random molecules colliding haphazardly in space? A slightly confused rider on the Great Mandala? Snakes and snails and puppy dog tails?

While struggling with these questions I came across a very helpful discussion of human nature in a book entitled *Renovation of the Heart* by Dallas Willard, a Christian thinker and professor of philosophy at University of Southern California. He finds six basic aspects that interact to form human nature:

1. Thought (image, concepts, judgments, inferences)
2. Feeling (sensation, emotion)
3. Choice (will, decision, character)
4. Body (action, interaction with the physical world)
5. Social Context (personal and structural relation to others)
6. Soul (the factor that integrates all of the above to form one life)

He explains, "Simply put, every human being thinks (has a thought life), feels, chooses, interacts with his or her body and its social context, and (more or less) integrates all of the foregoing as parts of one life. These are the essential factors in a human being."[10] He explains that in the context of the Christian ideal, the key is to understand how these various aspects of the self are effectively organized around God and restored and sustained in relationship to Him. This understanding offered me something like a picture on the cover of the puzzle box, a framework for approaching these broken bits of Humpty that are lying on the ground. Focusing on these different aspects and their interplay gave a context for understanding the dynamics at work in a spiritually abusive situation. Let's look at how each of these areas is impacted.

Thought: We've already discussed how thought life is heavily controlled in a cultic environment. To a certain degree it must be admitted that this also happens in society at large through various cultural influences and the religious environment (or lack thereof) in which one dwells. However, the unhealthy control of information and the short-circuiting of critical thinking in a high-control group is of an entirely different and more destructive order, as was brought out in our look at Steve Hassan's BITE model in the previous chapter.

Feeling: Willard points out that "the connection between thought and feeling is so intimate that the 'mind' is usually treated as consisting of thought and feeling together." In the damaged soul the mind becomes "a fearful wilderness and a wild intermixture of thought and feeling, manifested in willful stupidities, blatant inconsistencies, and confusion."[11] In the group, the emotional response to various stimuli is molded through deliberate manipulation. We believe we are "taking on the mind of Christ" and "bringing every thought into the obedience of Christ." In fact, the content and values we are so busy absorbing have been subtly relabeled, and the emotional response is modulated with a serious subwoofer dose of fear.

Will: In discussing the exercise of the will, Willard makes a point that seems critical to the whole issue of accountability. He connects freedom and creativity, two of the things most highly prized in human life, with the power of the will to do good or evil. This power belongs to each individual human. In order for this freedom of action to be truly our own, he explains, "there must be added to these conditions the inner and always unforced 'yes' or 'no' by which the person responds to the situation...It is ours; it is us, as nothing else is."[12]

This "inner and unforced" yes or no is exactly what so much of the cultic program seeks to eliminate and to replace with a conscience carefully shaped by the group's own values. In certain circumstances the control is so dominant and heavy-handed that the "unforced" qualifier cannot be fairly used.

The "unforced" piece here has become fairly central to the question of thought reform and behaviors in high-control environments. In a legal context the term "undue influence" figures into cases involving probate courts and the question of coercion in the signing of documents. These same issues have been hotly debated in a number of high profile cases such as the DC Sniper, the American Taliban, Patty Hearst, and others. Anyone who has had any firsthand experience related to cults can see clearly that many people do many things that would have been simply unthinkable to them without the massive influence of a totalistic environment, especially a religious one.

In thinking through this issue of human will, I went before the court of my own conscience and asked myself, "How do you plead?" I am sure that my inner defense attorney can make a decent case for some "diminished capacity" or some "mitigating circumstances" to soften things a little. I might try Eve's "the serpent beguiled me" or Adam's "the woman which thou gavest me causeth…" I do believe that the issues vary greatly in each specific situation. Ultimately, though, I don't think I am ready to view myself in a full-length mirror clothed only in a fig leaf. This is a multilayered issue, and I will dig at it a little deeper in the next chapter.

Body: This is where the rubber meets the road. "It is the body from which we live,"[13] observes Willard. Scripture describes the body as "the temple of the Holy Spirit." In the cult experience the walls of that temple are often profaned. In the Family the lack of boundaries in sexual matters is the most blatant of these trespasses. FFing and sexual sharing were not always completely voluntary activities, and were sometimes "encouraged" to the point of coercion. The boundaries of marriage, family, personal privacy, or even a reasonable concern for one's own health needs (diet, rest, and consistent medical attention) were often downplayed or ignored to the point of negligence, with severely detrimental results. It does not seem that this is what Jesus had in mind when He spoke of losing one's life to find it.

This aspect of "Body" in connection to the human personality goes beyond the physical ramifications of these abuses. Willard points out that our actions become habits that form character. Over time, this leads to a large percentage actions becoming a matter of habit. So what we do shapes who we are, and who we are determines what we do. The body eventually takes over many of our choices as a matter of habit, often with little or no reflection. It is not hard to see how this in-corp-orated (embodied) behavior can present a real challenge as we seek to break free from our "cult selves" on autopilot. It takes a careful and deliberate effort to sift through our habitual reactions and behaviors and reprogram our internal scripts.

Social Context: "The human self requires rootedness in others… we only live as we should when we are in right relation to God and to other human beings—thus the two greatest commandments,"[14] Willard observes. Cult life throws all of these relationships into a blender and flips it on *high*. From the description of our experiences, and their correlation to the breakdown described in the BITE Model, we can see how this group involvement reduces relationships to a pathetic puree, both with God and with the rest of humankind.

When we left the group this was one of the most difficult of all the aspects to which we struggled to adjust. Our "rootedness in others" was completely torn apart by the separation from almost all of the friends we had made in our adult lives. Beyond that, the whole template we had for interpersonal relationships was wildly distorted. Our roots had become seriously entangled with a whole host of invasive species that were choking off healthy growth. We could see that it was time for a transplant to a healthier ecosystem. However, communal living with all the uniquely intense experiences we had shared with others in the Family made the casual social connections we made in our new lives seem like pretty weak tea for quite a while.

Even attempts to establish new spiritual relationships were met with this type of challenge. I'll get into more about that issue later.

Soul: Willard writes: "The soul is that dimension of the person that interrelates all the other dimensions so they form one life...it is the deepest part of the self in terms of overall operations...It can be significantly 'reprogrammed.'"[15] This seems to me to be the most far-reaching impact of spiritual abuse on a person. Through gradual reprogramming of thoughts and feelings, the abuser deceptively establishes hegemony over the will and body. This "anti-Christ" (or "instead of Christ") belief system hijacks the soul. The scriptures speak of false spiritual systems making "merchandise of the souls of men." This is the "something" that "somebody stole."

So how are we to go about recovering our stolen property and return it to its rightful owner? Recognizing the aspects that go into the soul helped me to at least draw up a list of the missing items. As I went through the inventory it became clear that the process of repotting was not going to be quick and easy. It did help me to keep in mind that my plant was actually designed to thrive in a healthy natural environment. Much of the rest of the story will track our progress so far.

However, before we get too far into that process, I want to look a little more deeply at the questions of causes and accountability for the tangle of undergrowth we lived in for so long. Before replanting, it is necessary to clear the ground. If I wanted to own my future, I had to come to grips with and own my past.

CHAPTER 11

THE FELLOWSHIP OF THE WRONG

Sam: "Let's face it, Mr. Frodo... We're lost.
I don't think Gandalf meant for us to come this way."
Frodo: "He didn't mean for a lot of things to happen, Sam,
but they did."

~ from the film *The Two Towers*

One of the knottiest problems that one faces in the wake of a long-term commitment to a dream that turns into a nightmare is dealing with the inevitable questions of *why*. Ron Enroth comments in his book *Recovering from Churches that Abuse*:

Most people who are victims of spiritual abuse are sincerely seeking God. When they realize later that they have been involved in an unhealthy, abusive system, it is understandable that they may harbor resentment and bitterness against the leadership and against God himself. "Why did God allow this happen to me when I was sincerely trying to know His will?"[16]

The question arises again a little later in the book while addressing the stages of recovery:

SOMETHING SOMEBODY STOLE

Victims must be able to not only rebuild self-esteem and purpose in life, but also renew a personal relationship with God. That can be difficult for those who have yet to resolve the tough questions, "Why did God allow this to happen to me when I was sincerely seeking Him?" As one former church member puts it, "I had been taught that nothing was ever God's fault. The problem was that I was a true, believing Christian, but when I asked God for spiritual bread and water, look what I got. Was I praying to the wrong God? Was I dishonest? Secretly evil? Was I demonic, like the church kept telling me I was? How could an honest, sincere believer get tricked like this? How could God let this happen?"[17]

As I read through the literature about spiritual abuse, I continued to see the question posed repeatedly, but there seemed to be little attempt to actually answer it. There may be no easy answer, but it does seem that finding some peace in one's heart on this issue is essential if trust in the goodness and guidance of God is to be rebuilt. As in the story of Job, it wasn't really about getting a specific explanation as to the "why" of things, but rather to a fresh revelation that renews relationship.

The question of "How could God let this happen?" ties into the classic theological problem of evil. If God is good, why is there so much evil? There are entire shelves of books in theological libraries that deal with this matter from many angles, often arriving at different conclusions. I can only try to share briefly the thoughts that have been most helpful to me personally as I wrestle with this process.

First of all, the whole issue of our free will seems to be at the heart of the matter. If God is going to allow us the freedom to choose between right and wrong, then that in itself inevitably seems to open the door to things like deception, abuse, and pain. Once He'd established the ground rules on free will, it does sort of seem as though He puts some self-limitation on His intervention. (I realize this may be causing some Calvinists to go apoplectic, but what can I say? I guess I'm just predestined to believe in free will.) When it comes to allowing or not allowing things to happen, that's just how the principle of freedom at work in creation plays out. If you stop to consider the alternative, it does seem preferable to a creation populated by a race of preprogrammed automatons.

In the biblical record we are faced with the consequences of those very early free choices we find in the first few chapters of Genesis. We read that Adam and Eve had wonderful communion with the Creator, walking with Him in the garden in the cool of the day. Yet, even with their low-stress lifestyle in a paradisiacal garden and intimate personal fellowship with their Creator, they still fell prey to deception with the serpent's loaded language and ego stroking. The details of the account provide a treasure trove of archetypal insights into the nature of humanity's ongoing struggles from that point on. The first couple disrupts that unhindered fellowship with God by buying into the idea that they could be gods unto themselves. Things go downhill from there into egotism, jealousy, false worship, fratricide, and on into cities full of violence and confusion. Genesis continues to track God's initiatives to reach out to humanity through Abraham's family, but even these chosen vessels seem to be running around chaotically banging heads with each other and leaving messes on every other page. Oy vey. The rest of history is a pretty long string of "cults and isms" with a lot of resulting dysfunction and pain.

Thankfully, there runs a parallel line of liberating truth poking through the fog. Even since we moved out of the garden, we have struggled through this mix of good and evil, often inextricably intertwined. Church history certainly illustrates that pattern quite vividly. In one of His parables of the kingdom, Jesus tells this story:

The kingdom of heaven is like unto a man which sowed good seed in his field. But while men slept, his enemy came and sowed tares among the wheat, and went his way. But when the blade was sprung up, and brought forth fruit, then appeared the tares also. So the servant of the household came and said unto him, "Sir, did not thou sow good seed in thy field? From whence then hath it tares?" He said unto them, "An enemy hath done this."

SOMETHING SOMEBODY STOLE

The servants said unto him, "Wilt thou then that we go and gather them up?"

But he said, "Nay, lest while ye gather up the tares, ye root up also the wheat with them. Let both grow together until the harvest, and in the time of harvest will I say to the reapers, gather ye together first the tares and bind them in bunches to burn them, but gather the wheat into my barn."[18]

The coexistence of good and evil seems to be the reality we are faced with until the end of the age. This principle is at work not only throughout history in general, but even within each specific movement itself. Note the sentiments expressed in the letters to the churches recorded in Revelation chapters two and three. This was certainly my experience within the Family. Sorting the good from the bad is not only very tricky at times, but in some cases it may almost be impossible, at least from our current perspective, as the parable seems to indicate.

One day, many years after leaving the group, I was driving my youngest daughter and two eldest grandsons (all young teens at the time, very close in age to each other,) home from a weekend Christian youth camp. The conversation was about various ways people have of understanding the Bible, and the difficulty they had with some of the brimstone-tinged preaching they'd heard that weekend. This triggered a question from my daughter, fourteen years old at the time (she'd been only fifteen months old when we'd left the group): "Dad, if you knew then what you know now, would you have ever joined the Family?" After hedging a bit, explaining the impossibility of going back like that, I conceded that no, I suppose that I would not have. One of my grandsons quickly pointed out, however, that this would mean that they would not then even exist, thus illustrating the dilemma. Lots of good stuff, some of the best stuff in our lives, would never have happened. But neither would some of the worst.

Somewhere I read about the principle of the pearl. As most people know, the pearl actually begins as a bit of foreign matter that gets inside the shell of an oyster, irritating and endangering the soft internal flesh of the organism. To protect itself, the oyster coats the irritant with a smooth covering of nacre, or mother-of-pearl, layer upon layer, so as to prevent it from damaging the oyster's most vulnerable parts. Eventually, it becomes a thing of exceptional beauty. Perhaps there is a lesson there for us as well.

Throughout the Book of Genesis we read an amazing tale of family dysfunction and spiritual abuse. There are a number of doozies in there, but the longest story is the record of Joseph and his brothers. It is an interesting study in social psychology, but as most readers are likely to be somewhat familiar with the story, I will just quickly summarize. Joseph is sold by his jealous brothers into slavery in Egypt, where he is again unjustly framed and imprisoned. Due to his "excellent spirit" and spiritual gifts, he ends up in a prominent position in Pharaoh's court, where he saves Egypt from ruin at the time of a disastrous drought. The ensuing famine forces his brothers to come down into Egypt, seeking food, which puts Joseph in a position to perform of one of history's most famous acts of forgiveness, and to mercifully save his undeserving brethren and their families from starvation.

When the brothers are finally forced to face up to their crimes, Joseph, through his tears (the text reports he was "weeping loudly") comforts his brothers. He tells them that despite their ill intentions and his tragic ordeal, which had lasted years, God had a merciful plan through it all. After Jacob's death, Joseph has to reassure his worried brethren once again that he will not seek revenge with the expression: "Ye thought evil against me; but God meant it unto good..."[19]

There might be great benefit to be gained from Joseph's sense of perspective. His betrayal, enslavement, and unjust imprisonment were pretty tough, yet all of that adversity resulted in such a remarkable strengthening of his character and produced such a generosity of spirit that he is often spoken of as a foreshadowing type of Christ. His forgiving attitude serves as a model for how even the most awful experiences in life can be redeemed and point to a path of deeper understanding and a more compassionate outlook. If we recognize the inevitability of pain and sin in this fallen world and begin to open to positive outcomes that can flow from negative experiences, it can help us in the process.

When looking at the "why" factor in the case of involvement with destructive groups, the question of personal responsibility must also be seriously considered. The question may not be simply "how could God allow this?" I recall reading about a man who, while pondering all the sorrow and suffering in the world through war, oppression, poverty, and disease, turns to the Almighty and poses the oft-asked question, "God, how can You see all this horrible suffering in the world and not do something to stop it?" To which God replies, "How can you?" Ouch.

An earlier chapter looked at the ways destructive groups employ deceptive and manipulative tactics and the principles of thought reform in spinning the thought reform web. Certainly none of us answered an ad in the classifieds: "Zombies wanted to serve sacrificially in destructive cult. No salary. No benefits. New personality will be provided. Apply at...P.S.: Bring all your possessions with you to save time." Then again, most of us were not held at gunpoint either. So what about our responsibility?

Beginning in the Garden and down to the present, the serpent prefers subtlety to frontal assault. The snake is hip to what makes men tick. It is very hard, no matter how humanistic your perspective, not to hear a slight hiss and rattle in the background when the social psychology of cults is examined. Adam and Eve's attempts at shifting the blame simply did not wash. No "Twinkie defense" swayed the judge. They had to face up to the facts. They had made a few really, really bad choices.

I believe that most folks, including myself, who get hooked up with totalistic groups do so with sincere motives: to know, love, and serve God and to be a part of a movement that will bring salvation to many. The lifestyle is usually extremely sacrificial. I didn't stay at the Ranch in Texas, with its rustic accommodations and unique cuisine, for the perks. Yet, if I am rigorously honest with myself there were also some less than altruistic mechanisms at work. As Solomon put it, and he's a guy who oughta know, "There are many devices in a man's heart, nevertheless the counsel of the Lord, it shall stand."[20]

That spiritual classic that has captivated so many for the past several generations, *It's the Great Pumpkin, Charlie Brown!*[21] gives insight into this dynamic. Linus sacrifices an evening of trick-or-treating and the big Halloween party to keep vigil in the pumpkin patch awaiting the visitation of the Great Pumpkin, despite the scoffing of his relatives and friends. But Linus himself is clearly struggling with some niggling doubt of his own. In a reflective moment he unburdens his soul in hopes the Pumpkin hears: "Everyone tells us you are a fake, but I believe in you." Then as an afterthought he adds, "P.S....if you are a fake, don't tell me. I don't want to know."

That night he struggles with self doubt, as well as the doubts of his one convert, Sally, who spends part of the evening believing with Linus that they have "the most sincere pumpkin patch, and the Great Pumpkin respects sincerity." Sally defends Linus to the others: "Linus knows what he's talking about," and then to Linus she adds, "I hope so. I have my reputation to think about, you know!" Her crisis of faith intensifies as the evening wears on: "If anyone had told me I'd be waiting in a pumpkin patch on Halloween night, I'd have told them they were crazy." Finally, when she realizes all is lost and no Great Pumpkin with bags full of toys is going to show she bellows, "I was robbed! I spent the whole night waiting for the Great Pumpkin, when I could have been out for tricks-or-treats!"

Some of us can relate to Sally's roller coaster ride. Some of us can also relate to Linus in his exchange with Charlie the next day. Charlie tries to console him, "Don't take it too hard, Linus. I've done a lot of stupid things in my life, too." To which Linus erupts, "Stupid! Whaddya mean stupid? You just wait until next year, Charlie Brown!"

Good grief.

We finally came to admit to ourselves that we'd missed out on a lot of trick-or-treats and the big party and endured the scorn of our friends and the lonely chill of the night for naught. But what was even more devastating was coming to the sad realization that not only was no Great Pumpkin going to come bearing gifts, but that our own sincerity alone didn't cut it. Let's face it; I have to agree with Charlie: I did a lot of stupid things too. Even taking the "undue influence" issue into consideration, I have to admit that at least as our time in the group wore on, it wasn't always for the best of reasons. As James put it in his epistle, it's not God tempting us, but something coming from inside of us. Fear of missing out. Pride. Resisting the terrible letdown of admitting we were wrong. And lots of other nastier stuff. Writer and philosopher Neal Plantinga describes self-deception as "a mysterious process where we pull wool over our own eyes...We deny, suppress, or minimize what we know to be true. We assert, adorn, and elevate what we know to be false. We prettify ugly realities and sell ourselves the prettified versions."[22] This mechanism is known as cognitive dissonance. As one observer of human nature aptly put it: "We are all like the man on a diet who drove past the bakery and said he would only stop for doughnuts if there was an available parking space in front of it, clearly indicating that it was God's will that he eat a doughnut. Sure enough, his sixth time around the block a parking space opened up!"[23]

Thinking back through those years in the group and those moments of uncertainty and qualms of conscience that would surface at times of crisis and crossroads, I must admit I did my share of circling the block, waiting for the open parking space that would confirm that I was still on the right path. It's the old flipping a coin till we get the desired result: "best two out of three...OK, three out of five..." We are experts at talking ourselves into accepting the path of least resistance. If we really want the truth, we need to be willing to admit that our motives in the pumpkin patch were not always completely sincere.

M. Scott Peck addressed this need to "fess up" in his works *The Road Less Traveled* and *Further Along the Road Less Traveled*, from the viewpoints of both mental health and spiritual growth:

We live our lives in a real world. To live them well it is necessary that we come to understand the reality of the world as best we can. But such understanding does not come easily. Many aspects of the reality of the world and of our relationship to the world are painful to us. We can understand them only through effort and suffering. All of us, to a greater or lesser extent, attempt to avoid this effort and suffering. <u>*We ignore painful aspects of reality by thrusting certain unpleasant facts out of our awareness.*</u> *(emphasis mine.) In other words, we attempt to defend our consciousness, our awareness, against reality. We do this by a variety of means which psychiatrists call defense mechanisms.*[24]

In this context he invokes the Greek myth of Orestes, son of Clytemnestra and Agamemnon. Clytemnestra had taken a lover, and together they had murdered her husband Agamemnon. This put Orestes in a difficult bind, as it was the obligation of a Greek son to avenge his father's murder. At the same time, possibly the worst thing a Greek son could do was to murder his own mother. The old "damned if you do, damned if you don't." In the end, Orestes does kill his mother and her lover to avenge his father's death, but as a result he was cursed by the gods for this action, being haunted by the furies, three harpies who cackled in his ear, giving him hallucinations and driving him mad. For years Orestes wandered the world atoning for his actions, with the torment of the furies pursuing him. Finally Orestes asks the gods to relieve him of the curse. A trial was held and the god Apollo acted as his defense, arguing that the whole fiasco was actually the fault of the gods, as Orestes really had not had a choice in the matter and thus should not be held responsible. Orestes stood up to counter Apollo's argument, choosing to take responsibility, admitting, "It was I, not the gods, who murdered my mother. It was I who did this."

Never before had a human being assumed such personal responsibility for his action when he could have shifted the blame back to the gods! Hearing this, the gods were so impressed that they decided to lift the curse from Orestes. The Furies were then transformed into the Eumenides, which is translated literally as "bearers of grace." The nasty, incessant cackling was replaced with the comforting voices of wisdom. Peck observes the implications of the story: "This myth represents the transformation of mental illness into extraordinary health. And the truth is that the price of such a marvelous transformation is accepting the responsibility for ourselves and our behavior."[25]

On a slightly less lofty note, but along these same lines, in his contemporary classic "Margaritaville" Jimmy Buffet goes through various explanations for how exactly he landed in his frozen concoction–fueled

SOMETHING SOMEBODY STOLE

funk, searching for his lost shaker of salt. He starts out professing, "It's nobody's fault," progresses to "hell, it could be my fault," and finally arrives at, "but I know, it's my own damn fault." I'll drink to that.

Eventually, we need to face up to our personal responsibility (varying as it does—sometimes wildly—from case to case). This is the route out of "Margaritaville" and the path to freedom from the harping of the harpies. As one Psalm of David put it:

Count yourself lucky
how happy you must be—
You get a fresh start,
Your slate's wiped clean.
Count yourself lucky—
God holds nothing against you
And you're holding nothing back from Him.
When I kept it all inside,
My bones turned to powder,
My words became daylong groans.
The pressure never let up;
All the juices of my life dried up,
Then I let it all out;
I said, "I'll make a clean breast of my failures to God."
Suddenly the pressure was gone—
My guilt dissolved,
My sin disappeared.[26]

So why did God let it happen? To me, it is still not a neat little package. But these concepts have at least helped me to work through the issues. Like one of those stereograph "Magic Eye" pictures, perhaps not staring at any one set of dots is the key. As we pull the picture slowly back from our nose, the hidden image starts to come into focus.

It's a fallen world. And we all blow it. We need to see that reality. But we can still find a pearl if we look with the right kind of eyes.

CHAPTER 12

HEART OF DARKNESS

All orders were now issued through Squealer or one of the other pigs. Napoleon himself was not seen in public as often as once in a fortnight. When he did appear, he was attended not only by his retinue of dogs but by a black cockerel who marched in front of him and acted as a kind of trumpeter, letting out a loud "cock-a-doodle-doo" before Napoleon spoke. Even in the farmhouse, it was said, Napoleon inhabited separate apartments from the others. He took his meals alone, with two dogs to wait upon him, and always ate from the Crown Derby dinner service, which had been in the glass cupboard in the drawing room. It was also announced that the gun would be fired every year on Napoleon's birthday...Napoleon was now never spoken of simply as "Napoleon." He was always referred to in formal style as "our Leader, Comrade Napoleon," and pigs liked to invent for him such titles as Father of All Animals, Terror of Mankind, Protector of the Sheepfold...and the like. In his speeches, Squealer would talk with the tears rolling down his cheeks of Napoleon's wisdom, the goodness of his heart, and the deep love he bore to all animals everywhere.[27]

~ George Orwell, *Animal Farm*

Men never do evil so completely and cheerfully as when they do it from religious conviction.

~ Blaise Pascal

Clearly, there is really no "one size fits all" for measuring the damage one experiences in a group like the Family. There are many variables. When I hear about some people's experiences, even after having lived over twenty years in the group, much of it in leadership and in a wide variety of countries, I still find some accounts so horrific that they can be difficult to process. I have seen enough and heard enough corroborating testimony to realize that the whole movement became permeated to one degree or another with a very dark force. Some parts of it drifted into unspeakable evil.

It is not the aim of this book to try to convince anyone one way or another as to just to what degree or exactly how destructive the Family was or is. Some individuals, particularly some born and raised in the movement, experienced things clearly beyond the scope of this book's purview. Initially, I was hoping to avoid any in-depth discussion of this most sensational and catastrophic of all of the Family's abuses: the sexual abuse of children. Not only was I utterly intimidated by the scope of the subject, but I also felt woefully inadequate to the task. Due to events that have transpired since I first started writing this account, I realized that I needed to add a very difficult chapter to explore this aspect of the Family that has since become headline news. My objective in postponing this subject to a later part in the narrative is primarily in the hope of examining the issues in the context of my personal struggles and overall journey towards recovery.

Part of my purpose for writing this book was to try to supply some framework for a process of psychological and spiritual recovery from any aberrant Bible-based cult. Although I do this in the context of my own personal experience within a specific group, my hope is that it might offer insights that would prove helpful to others involved in very different groups, but faced with many similar challenges. This was my thinking as I struggled with how to approach this specific issue in the narrative.

In the next chapter I try to explore the issues that the first generation in general, and myself in particular, must struggle with concerning this weightiest of all matters faced by former members. But

HEART OF DARKNESS

I first want to try to return to exploring the dynamics that led to such a destructive environment in the first place. Those still in the group seem incapable of even recognizing how terribly wrong things have gone. For those of us who have at least gotten enough distance from the group to reevaluate our own experience, most would agree, things did indeed go terribly, terribly wrong. The question this chapter examines is: How did we get there? How did a journey to follow the light end up in such darkness?

We followed someone there.

Longshoreman philosopher Eric Hoffer published a best-selling study of the dynamics of mass movements back in the 1950s entitled *The True Believer*. Some of his conclusions are highly debatable, but some of his observations, which he applies to both political and religious movements, seem to provide a fairly accurate description of cult dynamics. (Interestingly, I have since learned from an early member that David Berg may actually have studied this text intently, and may well have drawn some strategic guidance from its pages. If true, this would have some pretty disturbing implications about Berg's intentions from the very early days of the movement.)

Hoffer discusses how there must be an intersection of the right circumstances and a leader with the unique mindset to spur fanaticism. "The leader cannot create the conditions to make the rise of a movement possible. He cannot conjure a movement out of the void. There has to be an eagerness to follow and obey, and an intense dissatisfaction with the way things are, before a leader can make their appearance..."[28]

The late 1960s was a time that produced an almost perfect growing environment for the rise of fanatical movements. The counterculture had produced a vast pool of disenfranchised youth, dropped out and frustrated with society's ills, as well as the failure of counterculture to bring about the peace and love it prophesied. Hoffer points out how the restless and dissatisfied "are receptive to the proselytizing movement." To provide the right material for a radical mass movement there must be the added ingredient of "those who crave to be rid of an unwanted self...it can satisfy the passion for self-renunciation...their imminent craving is for a new life, a rebirth..."[29]

This period produced one of the most far-reaching "revivals" in the recent history of Christianity, the Jesus Movement. The hunger for spiritual solutions was widespread. This factor also fed into that ideal matrix for new religious movements. When Hoffer's "men of words" came into this mix, cults sprang forth in abundance. Hoffer describes the emergence of this leader:

He articulates and justifies the resentment dammed up in the souls of the frustrated. He kindles the vision of a breathtaking future so as to justify the sacrifice of a transitory present. He stages the world of make-believe, so indispensable for the realization of self-sacrifice and united action...What are the talents requisite for such a performance? Exceptional intelligence, noble character, and originality seem neither indispensable nor perhaps desirable. The main requirements seem to be: audacity and joy in defiance, an iron will, a fanatical conviction that he is in possession of the one and only truth, faith in his destiny, a capacity for passionate hatred...a cunning estimate of human nature...unbounded brazenness which finds its expression in a disregard of consistency and fairness, a recognition that the inner most craving of a following is for communion and that there can never be too much of it, a capacity for winning and holding the utmost loyalty of a group of able lieutenants.[30]

Hoffer points out the dynamic interplay between leader and followers that feeds into fanaticism, focusing on the techniques for eradicating individualism to achieve mind-meld. He also points out how this can flow into an unquestioning unity, which in turn can lead to a dark tyranny.

Enter "Mo." David Berg seems to have been sent directly from central casting for the role of the quintessential cult leader. Tracking his psychological development would be a fascinating study on its own. Stephen Kent, a Canadian professor and researcher at the University of Edmonton, actually published a book-length examination of Berg's psychosexual history, gleaned primarily from Berg's own writings. There is, however, one specific psychological concept that helped a lot of puzzle pieces to fall into place for me.

Bob and Judy Pardon, the folks I introduced earlier, have studied and interacted with leaders and members of a wide variety of cults and have arrived at some interesting conclusions. In a handout (excerpted below) that they use at workshops they explain:

Many leaders of destructive groups (David Moses Berg, *Children of God;* Jim Jones, *People's Temple;* David Koresh, *Branch Davidians,* etc.) appear to be examples of a particular personality disorder called Narcissistic Personality Disorder. Clearly, not all suffering from Narcissistic Personality Disorders are leaders of destructive groups. However, in our experience, all leaders of truly destructive groups, if not true NPDs, exhibit extreme narcissistic traits and/or tendencies.

The DSM-IV, an official guide to diagnosis of disorders compiled by the American Psychiatric Society states: *"Many highly successful individuals display personality traits that might be considered narcissistic. Only when these traits are inflexible, maladaptive, and persisting, and cause significant functional impairment or subjective distress, do they constitute Narcissistic Personality Disorder."*[31]

Narcissism is defined as a pattern of traits and behaviors which signify infatuation and obsession with one's self to the exclusion of all others, and the egotistic and ruthless pursuit of one's gratification, dominance and ambition. It is described as an all-pervasive pattern of grandiosity (in fantasy or behavior), need for admiration or adulation, and lack of empathy. It usually begins by early adulthood and is present in various contexts. Five (or more) of the following criteria must be met. (All italicized descriptive quotes are from Dr. Sam Vaknin's definitive study, *Malignant Self Love: Narcissism Revisited.*)

1. Feels grandiose and self-importance (e.g., exaggerates achievements and talents to the point of lying, demands to be recognized as superior without commensurate achievements).

"The narcissist is prone to magical thinking. He thinks about himself in terms of 'being chosen' or of 'having a destiny'...He believes that his life is of such momentous importance that it is micromanaged by God...In short,

narcissism and religion go well together, because religion allows the narcissists to feel unique."[32]

2. Is obsessed with fantasies of unlimited success, fame, fearsome power or omnipotence, unequalled brilliance (the cerebral narcissist), bodily beauty or sexual performance (the somatic narcissist), or ideal, everlasting, all-conquering love or passion.

"The narcissist is haunted by the feeling that he is possessed of a mission, of a destiny,...that he is meant to lead, chart new ways, to innovate...to set precedents, to create. Every act is significant, every writing of momentous consequences, every thought of revolutionary caliber. He feels part of a grand design, a world plan..."[33]

3. Is firmly convinced that he or she is unique and, being special, can only be understood by, should only associate with, other special or unique or high-status people...

"The narcissist despises the very people who sustain his Ego boundaries and functions. He cannot respect people so expressly and clearly inferior to him, yet he can never associate with those evidently on his level or superior to him, the risk of narcissistic injury in such associations being too great."[34]

4. Requires excessive admiration, adulation, attention and affirmation—or, failing that, wishes to be feared and to be notorious (Narcissistic Supply).

"A common error is to think that 'narcissistic supply' consists only of admiration, adulation, and positive feedback. Actually, being feared or derided is also supply. The main element is ATTENTION...In short: the group must magnify the narcissist, echo and amplify his life, his views, his knowledge, his history..."[35]

5. Feels entitled. Expects unreasonable or special and favorable priority treatment. Demands automatic and full compliance with his or her expectations.

" He feels entitled to the best others can offer without investing in maintaining relationships or in catering to the well-being of his 'suppliers.'"[36]

6. Is "interpersonally exploitative"; i.e., uses others to achieve his or her own ends.

"He will not hesitate to put people's lives or fortunes at risk. He will preserve his sense of infallibility in the face of his mistakes and misjudgments by distorting the facts, by evoking mitigating or attenuating circumstances, by repressing the memories, or simply lying."[37]

7. Devoid of empathy. Is unable or unwilling to identify with or acknowledge the feelings and needs of others.

"Unable to empathize, he does not fully experience the outcomes of his deeds and decisions. For him, humans are dispensable...They are there to fulfill a function: to supply him with Narcissistic Supply (adoration, admiration, approval, affirmation, etc.). They do not have an existence apart from the carrying out of their duty."[38]

8. Constantly envious of others or believes that they feel the same about him or her.

"First there is pathological envy. The narcissist is constantly envious of other people: their successes, their property, their character...their spouses, their mistresses or lovers..."[39]

9. Arrogant, haughty behaviors or attitudes coupled with rage when frustrated, contradicted, or confronted.

"That which has cosmic implications calls for cosmic reactions. A person with an inflated sense of self-import reacts in an exaggerated manner to threats greatly inflated by his imagination and by the application of his personal myth...Narcissists live in a state of constant rage, repressed aggression, envy, and hatred. They firmly believe that everyone is like them. As a result, they are paranoid, suspicious, scared, and erratic."[40]

Conclusion:

"NPD is a pernicious, vile and tortuous disease, which affects not only the narcissist. It affects and forever changes people who are in daily contact with the narcissist."[41]

In my opinion, David Berg had all nine these criteria in spades. There is ample evidence of all these behaviors recorded in Berg's own writings. He often reflected back on his childhood, interpreting his loner instinct as a sign that God had singled him out for some great calling. He published many lengthy prophecies in which God confirms his calling as heir to the mantle of King David and others, but that his calling was greater than any who had come before. In one message he claims to be Aquarius—one doesn't meet a constellation every day of the week. He was convinced that the entire world thirsted for his "wonder working words." His spirit trips would occasionally indicate that even his bodily functions were fraught with great spiritual significance. (I will spare you the details.) He imagined himself the world's greatest lover—quite literally God's gift to women.

His behavior could be wildly erratic, ranging from expressions of tenderness toward the weak in his "Prayer for Love and Mercy" to bombastic strings of curses heaped on even his own daughter and granddaughter when he perceived any hint of disloyalty. On those occasions when I was in close proximity to him I felt a bit like a soldier gingerly picking his way through an Afghan village, never knowing where the next IED might be hiding. His radar was constantly on the sweep for any blip that he might interpret as a slight to his authority. Like King Saul, he was ready to hurl his javelin at any young David he jealously regarded as a potential threat to his complete control. He always seemed to have at the ready Moses's stone tablets, Samson's jawbone of an ass, Elijah's fire from heaven, or Elisha's hungry bears to guard his divine dignity. While I was on a visit to HQ as a representative from the mission field in India, I had passed along a question that had caused some confusion stemming from contradictory remarks in several of Mo's prophetic interpretations. His tape-recorded response was so explosive that Maria felt it necessary to preface it with a warning not to take it personally—it was just the way of the prophet.

I found it helpful to have a "name" for this type of personality, and one that fits his behavior so closely. It demystifies the actions, which while in the cult were shrouded in a pseudo-spirituality that was somehow designed to sanctify outrageous behaviors, and silence any voices of conscience that popped up within us as having been "a critical spirit," "rebellion," and the lies of Satan himself.

In his book *People of the Lie*, M. Scott Pack explores the connection between the psychological and spiritual dimensions in the area of evil.

> *The evil are pathologically attached to the status quo of their personalities, which in their narcissism they consciously regard as perfect...and it is out of their failure to put themselves on trial that their evil arises... The evil are "the people of the lie," deceiving others as they also build layer upon layer of self deception...A psychology of evil must be a religious psychology. By this I do not mean it must embrace a specific theology. I do mean, however, that it must...recognize the reality of the "supernatural"... according to the traditional Christian model, humanity (and perhaps the entire universe) is locked in a titanic struggle between the forces of good and evil, between God and the devil. The battleground of this struggle is the individual human soul.*[42]

If one accepts this worldview, it is fairly easy to understand why the spiritual forces of evil would zero in on those narcissists wandering around in the religious world and engineer a way to position them so as to influence a group of young idealists. These voices can then steer their followers away from their potential as a force for good and forge them into a zealous but misguided tool to sow confusion and harm. Once locked into this symbiotic relationship between leader and followers, there is a continuous cycle of the leader growing more and more tyrannical, unchecked in his proclivities and empowered by loyal followers. The movement consequently spirals further and further beyond the outer limits. Once utterly independent of mores constraining society, things can go unbelievably haywire without triggering as much as a whisper from anyone's conscience. Welcome to *The Island of Dr. Moreau*.

The seeds of Berg's eventual undoing were already present early in his history. It was quite a long journey from Berg's starting place as a fiery (though flawed) young evangelist to the narcissistic, hedonistic, manipulative megalomaniac that was to sow destruction in the lives of so many. From his own writings, it is clear he had long struggled with sexual sin, even crossing early on into the secret world of incest. It seems as though he may have channeled some of his own guilt feelings into a fanatical zeal, giving his preaching and teaching an aggressive, angry flavor. He quoted with pride a quilt-work portion of scripture-like "prophecy" that he felt described his calling: "a sharp-toothed threshing instrument to rip with violence the pillows from under the arms of those that dwell in ease in Zion." He focused intently on the failings of the established church, and energetically pursued TV and street evangelism with his own family while refusing to "touch the unclean thing" of the Great Whore Babylon religious system. Wrapping his identity in these illusory robes of righteousness may have helped him see his own moral failures as mere indiscretions. Later, he would go further, turning these vices into virtues, echoing in his life the words of Isaiah to backslidden Israel, "Woe unto them that draw iniquity with cords of vanity...that call evil good, and good evil: that put darkness for light, and light for darkness..."[43] How right Jesus was in warning: "Take heed therefore that the light which is in thee be not darkness...if therefore the light that be in thee be darkness, how great is that darkness!"[44]

A fellow ex-member told me that he had once spoken with a prominent Christian leader who as a young man in the Jesus Movement of the sixties had actually been present at the Christian coffeehouse The Light Club in Huntington Beach the night David Berg "declared war on the system," severing connections with the greater body of believers. This gentleman said he felt that what he had witnessed was a fulfillment of another scripture, this one from the book of Hebrews: "...Lest any root of bitterness springing up trouble you, and <u>thereby many be defiled</u>..."[45] (emphasis mine).

The Bible and history are littered with sad tales of lives that fall into ruinous darkness and madness. Still, these leaders often command large and loyal followings, which are simply unable to see behind the curtain. Hoffer wrote: "The fanatic cannot be weaned away from his cause by an appeal to his reason or moral sense. He fears compromise and cannot be persuaded to qualify the certitude and righteousness of his holy cause...He cannot be convinced, but only converted."[46]

This conversion to another holy cause is likely to be a rather hard sell to the refugees from Mo World, but breaking through the illusion of smoke and mirrors may take a conversion experience in itself. The wizard warns us to ignore the man behind the curtain, pulling feverishly at the controls, hoping that his desperate misdirection will somehow avoid his exposure. But to no avail. Truth, once seen, cannot be unseen. Lennon and McCartney may have captured something of the essence of the experience:

Your lips are moving, I cannot hear
Your voice is soothing, but the words aren't clear
You don't sound different, I've learned the game
I'm looking through you, you're not the same.
You're thinking of me, the same old way
Your were above me, but not today
The only difference is you're down there
I'm looking through you, and you're nowhere.[47]

Recognizing the truth about the source of darkness and staring at the pitiful pieces of shattered illusion that are scattered on the ground is at least a beginning. Jeremiah records the injunction, "to root out, tear down, destroy, and throw down..." as a necessary first step, but then we are told to "build and to plant."[48] Finding the direction and energy for this next step can prove to be even more difficult in the wake of such shocking disillusionment.

But before looking at new beginnings, I'd like to try to examine how the darkest of all the dark waters that sprang from this evil spring intersected with my own heart and life.

CHAPTER 13

SPEAKING OF THE UNSPEAKABLE

For it is a shame even to speak of those things which are done of them in secret.

~ Ephesians 5:12

I wrestled long and hard over the question of how address this thorniest and most disturbing of all the issues that swirl around the Family. Honestly, the issue of child abuse is so painful and troubling that it nearly stops me from even attempting to speak openly about my experience in the Family. In this day and age even the whiff of any involvement with the matter is enough to bring a person to public ruin. In the wake of the horrific scandals in the Catholic Church and the multitude of television exposés, it is not surprising that very few first generation Family members have been willing to even approach the topic publicly. Those few who have, to my knowledge, either do not have children or were no longer responsible for their care. Even without that primary consideration of any parent, the personal cost of addressing the subject has been great.

Admitting that this subject has come within a thousand miles of one's own family already opens all members, children and grandchildren included, to the inevitable conjectures of anyone who knows them, even many years after any involvement in the group. Even with the hope of aiding in the healing process of victims, the risk to one's own family is too great. A parent's protective instincts, especially in the wake of failures to do so while in the group, overrule any other consideration.

I need to preface this section with a quick affirmation that I was never personally involved in any sexual contact with a minor. I do not say that in order to in any way absolve myself from culpability for what happened in the group, but I am certain the reader will be asking that question and thought it best to get it out of the way.

Also, I want to clarify that I regard the issue of how those teachings may have affected any of my own children as completely off limits. Every member of the generation born and raised in the Family owns their own story, and I don't believe I, or any first generation (FG) ex-member, has the right to comment on any second generation's (SG) personal experiences. Those SGs who have felt the need have on occasion done so, often quite courageously in my opinion, in a number of public forums. Many others prefer to deal with it privately, seeking the path forward from their experience in whatever way seems most appropriate to their own situation. I admire each and every one of them, whatever their choice, and deeply and sincerely hope that they each can find healing.

But as a way of expressing the depth of the emotional turmoil that even approaching the issue raises for an FG adult, even many years after having denounced the group and its teachings, I will recount a personal experience.

In January of 2005, Ricky Rodriguez, (referred to at times by his former Family name, "Davidito") was involved in a very high-profile case of the tragic killing of an FG member followed by his own suicide. In the unlikely event that the reader is unfamiliar with these events, let me briefly recap.

Ricky was the son of Karen Zerby, known in the Family as Maria, who was, as mentioned earlier, the second wife of David Berg, the Family's late founder and leader. (In the wake of David Berg's death

Maria has become the group's leader, known as "Queen Maria," strange as that sounds. She is currently sharing the throne with her new husband, Steven Kelly, a.k.a. "King Peter," a long time member of Berg's inner circle who eventually rose to power at Maria's behest.) Ricky was born to Maria after one of her FFing trysts, and was raised in an inordinately publicized way, having had his childhood heavily photographed and documented in a series of internal Family publications known as "The Davidito Book." The group was offered glimpses of every detail of his peculiar upbringing as a sort of template to help us learn how to raise our children to be spiritual revolutionaries, specially prepared to lead God's people in the fast approaching End Times. (I know, it reads like the stuff of science fiction, but sadly, it is all too real.) We saw "Dito" involved in activities as innocuous as doing biblical flannel graphs, learning how to use a hammer, or do dishes. What is difficult to get your head around is the chronicling of what was labeled "love-up time" with his nannies. Published photos of this clearly would qualify as child pornography in many countries, and one would guess provide evidence sufficient to convict a number of people of child sexual abuse had they not been retouched to hide identities. Far from hiding this bizarre behavior, it was held up as a model. Like other aspects in Davidito's upbringing, it was to point a pathway to producing a generation that would be free from the sexual taboos of society, which had come to be viewed by Berg as satanic distortions of God's original purposes for sex. Its purpose was, in his view, complete uninhibited enjoyment of "the pure," with only a few practical rules with regard to health and security. (The one exception was male homosexuality, which was condemned.)

This became the catalyst for the eventual spreading of this horrendous practice of adult/child sexual contact to many segments of the movement for a number of years. Without a doubt, it was a clearly a devastatingly abusive experience for Rick personally. I had only brief contact with Dito when he was three or four years old, in a very innocuous setting, and found him to be exceptionally bright and well mannered. But what he must have been trying to sift through in terms of his deeper psychological development, I can only imagine. In fact, I actually can't imagine.

In the years that followed, Ricky went through various stages, and from what I can gather from what was publicized, by his early teen years he was starting to show signs of internal conflict. The Folks reacted to this in wildly erratic ways, swinging from mindboggling control to occasional loosening of the reins. Rick's occasional attempts to test the waters of even the most limited expressions of adolescent independence were met with public berating, sometimes published for the worldwide movement "that others also might fear."

Eventually Ricky began to break loose from the internal and external shackles forged by his environment. By his mid-twenties he had married and managed to leave the group with his wife. Like many other young people who had left, they struggled to adjust to life on the outside. As the true nature of how destructive his upbringing had been became clearer to Rick, he grew more focused in his anger towards his mother. (Berg had since died). Eventually, Rick and his wife separated. He reconnected with his mother's biological family in Tucson, and found a job and an apartment in that area. In 2005, Rick ended up crossing paths with Angela, one of his former FG caretakers, who had been involved in some of the adult/child sexual activities Mo and Maria had promoted in their household. He hoped to coerce Angela into revealing his mother's whereabouts. Within a few days, Rick had confessed to having killed Angela and then had taken his own life. He left behind a chilling videotape where with a hauntingly controlled rage he described his plans, 9-mm pistol and various other weapons on display, and explained his inability to continue on with his life. He had chosen to end it with a horrific act of revenge, followed by suicide.

News of this tragedy lit up ex-member Internet discussion boards, particularly movingon.org, which was the main site visited by SG survivors. Ricky's desperate act and its dire consequences became a catalyst for hundreds of intensely angry messages. Family leadership, including Ricky's own mother Maria, issued hollow and heartless "statements" to try and put their spin on these events. These self-justifying pronouncements sought to blame attacks on "bitter ex-members" and Rick himself. They were devoid of any sensitivity to the causes of the abuse-fueled rage with which Rick and many other Family-born young people seethed.

As we all know, the media lives for this sort of horror story, especially when set in the lurid backdrop of Berg's wildly illustrated sexual teachings and the group's high shock value. There was a rush of cable and network news teams to do extended pieces on their weekly news magazine programs, while the ink was still drying on the newspaper headlines. One major network, in an attempt to provide some context for the story, contacted Bob and Judy Pardon as widely recognized authorities in the cult recovery movement. They were asked if they could find an FG former member who would be willing to speak on camera to the issue from that perspective. Bob asked me.

We had always turned down requests to participate in any media coverage of the Family. Our primary concern was the impact that any fallout might have on our children (and grandchildren) who had now been leading mainstream lives of school, jobs, marriages, etc., for many years. Public discussion and resulting speculations could be at the very least a painful distraction, and given the cruelty of which school kids are capable, perhaps much worse. In addition, being in business for ourselves, it could only have a negative impact on our family's finances, which now were finally at least stable enough to pay the bills, though we still had a lot of catching up to do. On top of all of that, it was simply horrendously humiliating to admit to our former association with such a bizarre and screwed-up group.

On the other hand, the circumstances that surrounded Ricky's tragedy, and the aftermath among the second generation, were extreme. The Family was stonewalling, issuing wildly indefensible denials of reality in the face of articles and photos published about Ricky's childhood from its own publications. A significant number of SG survivors were speaking out to the press about their abusive upbringings. Discussions about the growing number of kids in dire straits, some even driven to suicide, could not help but weigh heavily on anyone who'd ever even helped to propagate the movement. The Family's infuriating denials and attempts to shift the blame onto the kids themselves were almost unbearable.

Most FG ex-members who participated in online discussion boards were highly sympathetic to the pain of the second generation and shared their outrage at the Family's insult-to-injury press releases. But the moral compromises we all shared at having been adults who joined this group by choice—whatever deceptions and manipulations had been involved—could not help but temper our indignation with shame. Other destructive teachings we had gone along with while in the Family all paled in comparison to this catastrophic debacle. No matter how well one grasps the dynamics of thought reform, it was simply an unavoidable fact: as a generation we had failed to protect our children.

What created a real moral dilemma for me personally with regard to this interview request is that it seemed that no FG voice that had been active in the group during the period of the worst abuses was speaking in the public media to validate the charges being made by an increasingly irate SG population. In the end, one brave former leadership insider did, at great personal cost, agreeing to be interviewed in silhouette in support of the SG's charges. I was not aware of this while struggling with the decision of whether to be interviewed or not. It may have served to let me off the hook.

For the next thirty-six hours I tossed and turned the question over and over in my mind. I was swimming in a soup of grief, fears, shame, anger, compassion, and confusion, barely able to keep my head above water. I tried to pick up guidance from my wife, kids, friends, and God, but the emotional turmoil made it impossible to come to a peace. In the end, I think I made a decision based more on a gut reaction, the sort of impulse that makes you intervene when you see someone being bullied, even if you know that is likely to be you that will end up lying on the ground with blood oozing from both nostrils. Despite the risks to my family and myself, I felt that for whatever it was worth, I needed to stand up and say that the Family was simply lying, and the SG community was speaking the truth, much to my personal shame.

The network agreed to shoot me in silhouette, although as anyone who has watched such interviews on TV knows, your identity is likely to be recognized by people who know you. The interviewer seemed to have a grasp of the basic dynamics of cult thought reform from conversing with Bob, and had a calming and sympathetic demeanor. While the camera crew set up in the hotel suite where the interview was to take place, the producer had us watch Ricky's video for the first time. It was both chilling and deeply upsetting. They had agreed not to ask me any questions about my own family, as I'd insisted, for reasons already explained. But despite this stipulation, the emotions that surfaced inside of me were deeply personal. The tremendous pain of the collective second generation hit me directly in the solar plexus. Their suffering seemed to come into my consciousness as though it were the suffering of my own kids. Several times during the interview there were long, silent pauses. My emotions would simply paralyze me. I couldn't form words. I could barely breathe.

After we were done, the interviewer and producer both thanked me sincerely, understanding how upsetting the whole thing was and recognizing the difficultly I was having over the whole confusing mess. The piece, I realized, would probably be edited down to at most a quick sound bite to provide minor background to the story. The story would obviously spotlight the grisly and sensational aspects of the event. But for the next few days I was shaking. I could barely sleep, awaking to nightmares and cold sweats. I was leaving messages with the producer trying to find out what was going on with the piece, when it would air, etc. I was a disaster zone.

In the end, the network did not use the clip. You cannot imagine how greatly relieved I felt. Although I did wish there was some way that I could support the SGs, I was (whatever this says about me) really thankful that the result of my gut reaction did not end up with my nose bleeding in the dirt.

So why do I share all that, despite the fact that I realize the overall picture is less than flattering to me personally? Clearly, my personal issues and struggles are of an entirely different nature than those of a young SG trying to overcome a traumatic and abusive upbringing. I'm not trying to say I can even begin to understand how any one of them must feel. (Although through close personal experience I have had to learn a little about the interior landscape of trauma victims.) But I say all of that simply to lay out for any SG reader that your struggles affect me deeply. As an FG former member I feel deep shame about your experience. I am deeply, deeply sorry for how we as a generation, and myself as a parent, simply failed.

How could we...I...allow myself to remain connected to a group that taught and practiced such things? How could any responsible adult fail to protect or try to intervene? How could any of us stand by and allow these travesties to proceed unchallenged?

That may be the most difficult question of all. I've already explained from my perspective how the dynamics of social psychology can gradually redefine one's understanding of reality in terms completely outside any reference to mainstream societal attitudes, or normal sense of morality. There was a powerful conviction that the world was out of sync with the Creator on almost every issue of life, and we alone were yielded enough to His will to understand His true heart on all these issues. I do realize how horribly empty this sounds now, but I did not then.

I have already expressed my struggles with David Berg following my visit to his HQ in France. Much of this abuse came to light after this crack had already appeared in the dyke of my faith. Why didn't I break free then? Why couldn't I allow the blinders to come off completely, at least by that time?

I will share one more personal story that might help the reader to at least begin to understand. I do not ask anyone to excuse. None of this in any way excuses these choices, or else there are no grounds for anyone to be held morally accountable for anything. But I think that this illustration might help shed some light.

After our public demotion and denouncement back in the late seventies, my family went back to Asia for another year. We were still reeling emotionally and spiritually from these events, but appreciated being out of the Family mainstream and the scrutiny of leadership. We attempted to get long-term residence visas by starting a business partnership with another (somewhat independent) brother and a Sri Lankan national. Eventually the paperwork stalled and we were forced to leave Asia. We ended up spending a year back in the States. Here we not only grew more independent (the US being loosely supervised at the time) but began developing closer relationships with other sincere and committed Christians. We were getting a broader exposure to the mindset of mainstream Western culture, as well as biblical viewpoints that called some of ours into question. At one point I began to express some doubts about certain of Berg's doctrines to my wife. Being a faithful disciple, more preoccupied with issues of child rearing and survival, she had no time for my "double-mindedness" and rebuked me for opening up to Satan's voice, and let me know I had better get right quickly, or else! Knowing well that "the heart is deceitful above all things and desperately wicked, who can know it?"[49] and knowing my own capacity for doubt, I tried hard to chase my thoughts back into line. From that time on though, it remained a constant, if silent, battle.

Eventually we ended up teaming up with some other brethren and traveling down to a remote section of Mexico to return to missionary life. At the time we were camping in a beautiful but primitive spot, when my six-month-old daughter got sick. After taking her to the hospital, we learned that she had contracted whooping cough, which had quickly led to double pneumonia. It is almost unbearable to watch a tiny six-month-old baby struggling for each breath. Life seemed to be ebbing from her by the minute. As she lay in the oxygen tent unconscious and barely moving, I felt as though I were watching her spirit slip out of her body. I left the emergency room, and in the middle of the night I knelt on the hospital floor, crying out to God with every ounce of strength and faith I could muster.

I earnestly repented of any sin that might have invited such judgment on my family. When you see your baby daughter at the very precipice of death, believe me, you are willing to confess to anything and accept anything that you feel may clear the way to her healing.

Without trying to explain the details, through a sense of unusual signs and scripture passages that I received during that desperate time of crying out to God, I became convinced that my sin was allowing myself to doubt God's Prophet. I wept bitterly, feeling like Peter after having denied the Lord three times. I pledged that I would henceforth yield and obey, and be a loyal disciple, submitting to His Prophet.

Immediately my baby began to regain a little strength. Within a few hours she was moved from the ER to an intensive care unit. In Mexico parents were allowed (and expected) to maintain round-the-clock watch and care for sick children. Her mother and I rotated on and off running a nebulizer, administering medications, comforting little Maggie as we patted her back vigorously to break up congestion, and changing her diaper often due to the diarrhea the antibiotics were causing. We rocked, sang, bounced, and prayed nonstop for a week. During this time we received a mailing from the Family with a revelation based on Mo's latest dream. It was called "Keep on Believing." Its message was basically that if you had missed some important calling due to hesitation or unbelief, you could still get the next bus. But you had to jump on without hesitation or question, in loyal obedience and complete trust. Just a few days later, while still in that broken state, I received a telegram from the Family's HQ in Mexico asking me to take a thirty-six-hour bus ride to attend a leadership meeting at the personal invitation of Mo's daughter Faithy. As Faithy had been the one who previously demoted me, it seemed to be an almost literal fulfillment of the "Keep on Believing" letter. It seemed to be a gold-embossed personal invitation from God Himself for me to forsake my independence and redeem myself through "jumping on the bus" without hesitation and rejoining the ranks of the loyal.

I share all of that to set the stage for my arrival at HQ. Shortly after being welcomed back I was once again confronted with the obvious signs of some adult/adolescent sexual contact. (Things like this did seem to appear when Faithy visited during that era, as she saw herself as bringing "the spirit of David" to each field.) But still shaken from the near loss of my daughter, and convinced that I was being given sign after sign that I was simply to follow without question (with potentially dire consequences for my little ones if I did not!) I was incapable of evaluating the moral issues involved in any logical way. Thankfully, I was at least spared the devastation of ever being coerced manipulated to partake of this tragic practice.

It is difficult, as a believer, for me to explain how this series of events and coincidences seemed to have aligned to convince me, against my natural inclination, to return to the mindset of a loyal disciple of Berg. I will tell you that I approach divine guidance much more cautiously and circumspectly now. (I have since learned that this confused interpretation of the causes of events, attributing them to God's actions, is common in abusive groups, and is called "misattribution.") Please understand, I am not trying to excuse my choices. But perhaps it may explain why a person who in other ways seems to reflect a fairly normal set of human reactions could possibly misjudge something so blatantly obvious to most.

There are a significant number of personal stories of SGs from this time period who experienced a variety of abusive situations, sexual and otherwise. There are also numerous stories of FGs and SGs who never personally witnessed these practices in their locations. Some accounts clearly point to the actions of obvious pedophiles that saw this highly sexualized and permissive atmosphere as an invitation to feed their bent impulses. There are also stories of adults who were reluctantly manipulated into compromising situations and gave in, deluded that God was asking it of them. Either way, from an SG perspective, the end result is still the trauma of childhood sexual abuse, and sometimes a life burdened with profound psychological struggles.

There is no excuse. We have no excuse. I have no excuse. For my role I am deeply, deeply sorry...for whatever little that is worth.

It was a gradual process to begin to realize just how devastating this mess has been in so many lives. It is still difficult, even given my own experience of thought reform and spiritual delusion, and what is now well over a decade of study, research, and dialogue, to try to understand these issues. Learning how such trauma can devastate a child and leave him or her facing a long struggle to recover leaves me searching for ways to somehow try and contribute to any healing available. I certainly do not have the answers. But I do believe there is hope and help available.

If anyone reading this has been affected by this tragedy is searching for help, I invite you to contact Bob or Judy Pardon. Over the last few years they have pioneered a transitional program that has helped many victims of abusive high-control groups, including a number of ex-Family SGs (www.meadowhaven.org). It is no surprise that sexual abuse is often intertwined with cultic spiritual abuse. They have gained a great deal of insight into these issues, as well as the healing and recovery process, and have a thorough grasp of the Family's history in this regard. You will be welcomed warmly.

Somehow, I'm going to try to get back to the rest of the story...

CHAPTER 14

YOUR GOD IS TOO WEIRD

God made man in his image...and man returned the favor.

~ Blaise Pascal

It is always true to some extent that we make our images of God...It is even truer that our images of God make us. Eventually we become like the God we imagine.

~ Brennan Manning, *The Lion and the Lamb*

In the previous few chapters I wrestled with the question of why I had invested so much of my life in what ended up being a destructive movement. The fallout from the cult experience has continued to shape the landscape of my family's continuing journey at almost every turn. The stresses of parenting a large family with limited financial resources can be daunting enough. Having ghosts from our past pop up every few feet like animatrons in a theme park house of horrors made the trip not only more exhausting but also made the effort to understand the terrain an urgent matter of survival. This was not a purely academic exercise.

At the center of these real-life issues was the whole question of God. After the demoralizing experience of spiritual abuse it is not surprising that a good many ex-members choose to simply change the channel. Not only can "God talk" be contradictory and confusing, it also seems that many of those doing the talking are only loosely connected to reality. In addition, they are too often just not very nice people. If, as the Gospels profess, "by their fruits ye shall know them," many of religion's loudest voices ought to be avoided like those suspect peaches in the reduced-for-quick-sale shelf at the market. It is no wonder that some may want to check out the other aisles. I don't blame anyone who feels the need to slide theological questions to the back burner as they seek distance from the pain of the reentry process. As those pesky tiles on the space shuttle heat shields can testify, reentry can be pretty stressful.

Unlike many of my fellow travelers, however, I was incapable of putting a hold on the need to find a fresh spiritual perspective from which to live. It wasn't a question of how many angels fit on the head of a pin. God had been the glue that held our marriage together. He had given us our daily bread. He had been the source we looked to in every decision of our lives. We had no other default setting to which we could revert. Somehow we needed to get a hold of God in a new way. We needed to be born again—again.

Perhaps it will seem illogical or even self-delusional to some, but I remained unshaken in my commitment to Jesus. Whatever tectonic plates had shifted under my feet, I was not even thinking about rethinking the core Christian story. I had allowed its message to be messed with and found much of what I'd figured for faith to be foolishness, but I was still convinced of my conversion. Philosophical and psychological questions of why we believe what we believe hadn't yet figured into my thinking. (I've had to seriously grapple with these issues since, due to a long-running dialogue with a particularly well-read skeptic who also happens to be one of my sons.) I was, at the time, probably capable of offering a moderately coherent defense of the reasons for the hope that was in me, but really, if pressed, it boiled down mostly to "I know it in my knower."

The religious impulse of humanity runs deep. St Augustine famously observed, "Thou hast made us for Thyself, O Lord, and our own hearts are restless until they find their rest in Thee." And Pascal chipped in: "There is a God shaped vacuum in the heart of every man which cannot be filled by any created thing, but only by God, the Creator." I was acutely aware of my own "restless heart" and "God-shaped vacuum." My security blanket cult faith was now little more than a tattered rag. However, the shortest route to an unclouded view of the one true God and His perfect will did not seem to be clearly mapped out in my Lonely Planet guidebook. I felt like I was almost back at the beginning of my story, once again hunting for clues.

I found myself relating to the Old Testament character Job. In scripture we see him reeling under the weight of the tremendous loss of all that he held dear. Bereft of fortune and children and covered with boils from head to toe, Job "took him a potsherd to scrape himself withal: and he sat down among the ashes." His wife advises him to "curse God and die," a path of action no doubt considered by more than a few spiritual abuse victims. Then his counselors basically blame Job for his mess, certain that his woes are the result of his own secret sins. Again, this is a situation to which many ex-members can probably relate. Good counsel can be tough to find.

Finally, in a great struggle of soul, Job decides to spill out his whole case to God Himself. In an argument not far from what one might hear from someone still stinging from the thwack of exiting a cult, Job asks: "How could God, in whom I put my trust and sought to serve with all my heart, let me go through all this?" God chooses not to address the specific issues in the way Job sought, but rather chose to answer "out of the whirlwind" with a fresh revelation of His being, blowing away the previous woefully inadequate images of Him held by Job and argued for by his friends. Like Job, among the broken pieces of my life I sought a new vision. My search led me to public libraries and book sections of Goodwill stores. A handful of nuggets emerged, providing me with a few insights.

In his bestselling book from the 1970s entitled *The Road Less Traveled*, noted psychiatrist M. Scott Peck points out the connection between one's concept of God and mental health. In his counseling practice he often encountered what he came to call "the monster-god." This concept had been instilled in his patients by extremely strict, legalistic religious upbringings coupled with harsh parenting. "I used to tell people facetiously that the Catholic Church provided me with my living as a psychiatrist," he quipped, adding that the same could be said of many other churches as well. In the case of many cults, the truth of this could be multiplied many times over, though it seems doubtful that many could afford the therapy! In a section of his book aptly titled "The Baby and the Bathwater," Peck examines the question of God's character in a historical context:

There is clearly a lot of dirty bathwater surrounding the reality of God. Holy Wars. Inquisitions. Superstitions. Stultification. Dogmatism. Ignorance. Hypocrisy. Self-righteousness. Rigidity. Cruelty. Book-burning. Witch-burning. Inhibition. Fear. Conformity. Morbid guilt. Insanity. The list is almost endless. But is all this what God has done to humans, or what humans have done to God?[50]

A few paragraphs later he concludes:

There is reason to believe behind spurious notions and false concepts of God there lies a reality that is God. This is what (theologian) Paul Tillich meant when he referred to the "God beyond God," and why some sophisticated Christians used to proclaim joyfully, "God is dead. Long live God![51]

British theologian (and friend of C.S. Lewis) J.B. Phillips frames the issue with crystal clarity in his powerful little classic, *Your God*

Is Too Small. He writes, "It is obviously impossible for an adult to worship the conception of God that exists in the mind of a child of Sunday school age, unless he is prepared to deny his own experience."[52] He goes on to methodically lay out to view many of the "small gods" that occupy the religious beliefs of so many:

"Resident Policeman" (restricting God to mere conscience.)

"Parental Hangover" (God as a slightly bigger earthly father.)

"Grand Old Man" (an old-fashioned relic, out of touch with today.)

"Meek and Mild" (the soft and sentimental Jesus. Fetch a doily.)

"Absolute Perfection" (and He demands it of you too!)

"Heavenly Bosom" (the god of escape.)

"God-in-a-Box" (available only to members.)

And the list goes on: "Managing Director," "Second Hand God," "Perennial Grievance," "Pale Galilean," "Projected Image," and "Assorted"—just to cover all bases.[53] (David Berg added a few new wrinkles, investing God with his own sexual proclivities and narcissistic tendencies.)

The point, of course, is that it is wise and necessary to dump these poor excuses for the Almighty. Phillips doesn't stop there. In the second half of the book he examines the question of an adequate God. "Let us fling wide the doors and windows of our minds and make some attempt to appreciate the size of God," he writes. He then goes on to build a case, brick by brick, for a fresh, free concept of the God that is actually pointed to in scripture, available to our experience, and sufficient to our need.

In the aftermath of the cult experience one's image of God is usually shattered. The God of small, high-control groups takes on the nature of almost a local tribal deity. You get the impression that His list of things to do is mainly centered on the daily affairs of your own little group, with perhaps a few items way down the page concerning the rest of Christendom and keeping the universe spinning. We make our own images of God…and ours began to bear a striking resemblance to the Family's own "Prophet and Founder."

SOMETHING SOMEBODY STOLE

There is an image that captures the essence of this situation in the final volume of C.S. Lewis's Narnia series, *The Last Battle*. In the story, a manipulative ape aptly named Shift and a rather simple-minded donkey, Puzzle, happen upon the skin of a lion floating in a river. Shift develops a rather elaborate scam, cloaking Puzzle in the lion skin and parading him at night, illumined only by shadowy firelight, purporting to the unsuspecting that this was the "Great Aslan" (the Christ figure/lion in the Narnian tales). Shift manages to milk this ruse for all it is worth, even going so far as to strike an unholy alliance with the dark forces of an enemy kingdom, with disastrous results.

Narnia's good, young King Tirian and a few loyal friends eventually discover the plot and succeed in capturing the hapless donkey with the purpose of exposing the charade and rallying the captive subjects of Narnia to fight for their freedom in the name of the true Aslan. The first party they come upon is a band of Narnian Dwarfs marching to slavery in the neighboring, conquering kingdom. The king and his friends expose the masquerading donkey and defeat the enemy guards. Tirian then attempts to enlist the newly liberated Dwarfs in the freedom fight. The king and his heroic helpers are shocked to find the Dwarfs not only reluctant to join the battle, but actually hostile to any suggestion that the true Aslan "is on the move."

One of the gruffest of the Dwarfs, Griffles, grumbles:
"You must think we're blooming soft in the head, that you must....We've been taken in once, and now you expect us to be taken in again the next minute. We've no more use for stories about Aslan, see? Look at him! An old moke with long ears!"
Tirian replies:
"Which of us said THAT was Aslan? That is the Ape's imitation of the real Aslan. Can't you understand?"
"And you've got a better imitation I suppose!" said Griffle. "No thanks. We've been fooled once and we are not going to be fooled again."

After further discussion along these lines, with Tirian and Jill going to great pains to try and help the Dwarfs grasp the difference between the fraud they'd just experienced and the true Aslan, emotions continue to escalate. Finally the Dwarfs adamantly proclaim:

"We're on our own now. No more Aslan, no more kings, no more silly stories about other worlds. The Dwarfs are for the Dwarfs." And they began to fall into their places, and to get ready for marching back to wherever they came from...[54]

It is not hard to understand the feelings of the Dwarfs. The tendency to want to dump the whole subject of God is indeed strong after leaving a cult. For this very reason it seems wise to recognize the reaction and avoid a precipitous judgment using faulty criteria. But is it possible to reexamine issues of faith without getting drawn into another ape and donkey show?

Ironically, the answer might just appear riding on a donkey. The triumphal entry of Jesus into the city of Jerusalem on Palm Sunday (described in Matthew chapter 21) must have been an incredible rush for his disciples. It had been tough following the Master, and they had been through a lot of rejection. But now folks were finally beginning to recognize Him as the Messiah, and they were in the inner circle! Visions of grandeur blossomed as they started seeing themselves in various key positions in the "next administration." Their expectations, however, did not include the ignominy and torture he was to receive only a few days hence. Their imaginings were soon to come crashing down around their ears, ending with the utterly unfathomable fact of His dead body lying in the grave of a secret friend. The disciples, who only a few days earlier had been squabbling over positions in the new kingdom that their Master, it seemed certain, was soon to usher in, were now huddled in a room behind locked doors "for fear as they mourned and wept." When they received early reports of His resurrection from several of his most devoted female followers, they scoffed at them as "idle tales," perhaps the product of emotionally unstable minds unable to deal with the harsh new reality.

SOMETHING SOMEBODY STOLE

It is easy to sense of the deep disillusionment His followers felt from a passage in the Luke's Gospel (chapter 24) in which he recounts the story of two of Jesus' followers departing from Jerusalem in the wake of the catastrophe. Disconsolate, they walked along, grieving not only the death of the Master but also the shattering of their own hopes and dreams. As they dragged themselves down the road in this state, Luke tells us that Jesus drew near, "but their eyes were holden, that they should not know him." (Pain can do that to a person.)

At this point Jesus spoke to them: "What manner of communications are these that ye have one to another as ye walk, and are sad?" They answered, perhaps a little impatiently, "Art thou only a stranger in Jerusalem and hast not known the things that are come to pass there in these days?" Then Jesus began to open to them the scriptures, which offered a completely fresh understanding of these events in the light of the plan that had long been foretold concerning the Messiah. Still not recognizing Jesus in His resurrected state, yet with their hearts "strangely warmed" by His words, they pressed Him to stay with them for a meal. It was only something in the way He broke the bread and blessed it that finally triggered their recognition of who He was for a brief moment, and then He again disappeared!

Meanwhile, back at the ranch, the disciples who were gathered in Jerusalem were starting to come out of their deep grief and consider a growing number of unexplained reports of the Master's appearances. As the first rays of hope stirred again within them that perhaps all is not lost, the almost unbelievable happened! "And as they thus spake, Jesus himself stood in the midst of them, and saith unto them, 'Peace be unto you.'" Peace seems an unlikely reaction. Luke goes on to report, "But they were terrified and affrighted and supposed that they had seen a spirit." Most of us can relate to that sort of skeptical response. Jesus spoke again: "Why are ye troubled? And why do thoughts arise in your hearts?" And Jesus went on, inviting them to examine the evidence: the fresh scars in His hands and feet. He again proceeded to try to straighten out their misconceptions about who

He was and the plan they had failed to recognize spoken of throughout the scriptures. Most of them could probably quote many of the relevant passages by heart, but they had failed to connect the dots, because they were, as Jesus puts it, "slow of heart."[55]

Like the disciples, or perhaps the Dwarfs, I was challenged to a painful reexamination after my experience with "the monkey and donkey." Should we march off with the Dwarfs, "looking out for ourselves from now on?" Or perhaps we would be wiser to linger awhile before drawing any permanent conclusions. You never know who might show up as we "walk, and are sad," or perhaps even drop in for dinner.

Some dinner guests, though, can leave a bad taste in your mouth. It might take a little while to figure out exactly who you want to include on your guest list. Popular Christian author Phillip Yancey tells of his utter disillusionment with Christianity after being raised in an abusive, racist, and dysfunctional fundamentalist church in the segregationist South of his childhood:

Although I heard that "God is love," the image of God I had from sermons more resembled an angry, vengeful tyrant...Ever since I have been on a quest to unearth the good news, to scour the original words of the gospel and discover what the Bible must mean by using words like love, grace, *and* compassion *to describe God's character. I sensed truth in those words, truth that must be sought with diligence and skill, like the fresco masterpieces beneath the layers of plaster and paint in the ancient chapels.*[56]

The Jesus found in the Gospels is full of compassion and a friend of the suffering. He connects with folks who find themselves on the outs—the poor, the prostitutes, the drunks, the moral failures, the broken in body and soul. Very early in Jesus' public ministry he reads from the scroll of Isaiah: "The Spirit of the Lord is upon me because he has anointed me to preach the gospel to the poor, he hath sent me to heal the broken hearted, to preach deliverance to the captives and recovering of sight to the blind, to set at liberty them that are bruised." Jesus announces that this prophecy is fulfilled in Him, making this His mission statement, and one that He lived up to throughout his ministry. These activities did not endear Him to society's upper echelons, but He stuck with his program to the end, comforting the afflicted and afflicting the comfortable.

Ironically, cult leaders often manage to turn this imagery on its head. David Berg had initially invoked the rebel Jesus to connect with the revolutionary impulse of the youth of the 1960s. Yet within a few short years, the religious leaders against whom we'd rebelled were replaced by some of those same rebels who, in turn, took the tools of spiritual control to a whole new level. Some of the barnyard crew from *Animal Farm* were soon ensconced in the farmer's house and were quick to surpass the abuses of the prior occupant. (I had eaten off the farmer's fine china several times myself.)

A perfect example of this upside-down approach to interpretation can be found in several of the very passages that were cited to support Berg's "unique calling" and authority—the so-called "David" prophecies in Ezekiel and Jeremiah. These messages originated at a time when Israel is in exile, scattered and defeated as a result of the corruption of its leadership. The prophets bring a stinging rebuke to these false shepherds: "The diseased have ye not strengthened, neither have ye bound that which was broken, neither have ye brought again that which was driven away, but with fierceness and cruelty ye have ruled them. And they were scattered because there is no shepherd...Seemeth it a small thing unto you to have eaten up the good pastures? And to have drunk of the deep waters? As for my flock, they eat that which ye have trodden with your feet, and drink that which ye have fouled with your feet?"[57]

There may be no better description of the way scripture-twisting cult leaders end up polluting the green pastures and still waters, leaving their followers splattered with mud. It is downright weird that we somehow applied these passages to the corrupt leaders of "churchianity" but failed to see that the new regime had become two-fold a child of hell.

Ezekiel continues: "For thus saith the Lord God: Behold I, even I, will both search my sheep and seek them out...As a shepherd seeks his flock in the day that he is among his sheep that are scattered in a cloudy and dark day...Because ye have thrust with side and shoulder, and have pushed all the diseased with your horns till ye have scattered them abroad, therefore will I save my flock and they shall be no more a prey."[58] Rather than this rescue being fulfilled by Moses "David" Berg, as we had accepted, he turned out to be the one doing most of the pushing and shoving! The rescue was actually fulfilled through the ministry of Jesus, the "Son of David," the one "anointed" as described in His quoted mission statement and described again in several key gospel passages. (See Matthew 9:36 and John 10:1-16.)

Just as J.B. Phillips dismisses the too small gods earlier on, I felt the need to shoo away the false christs and false apostles. I gathered together all the pretenders to the throne—the Great Santini father figures, the sweaty-palmed Elmer Gantry of Nazareth, the foaming-at-the-mouth Reverend Ayatollah, the bobble-head Jesus doll with position papers on everything from apocalyptic scenarios to IRS tax codes—and escorted the whole ghastly Halloween party to the door marked "weeping and wailing and gnashing of teeth" and closed it firmly behind them. I hoped that once all that clatter died down it might be possible to hear the gentle knocking of another, waiting patiently to come in, sit down, and have an honest conversation over a friendly falafel.

CHAPTER 15

HOW FIRM A FOUNDATION?

There's a moment when all things
Become new again
But that moment might have come and gone
All I have and all I know
Is this dream of you
Which keeps me living on

~ Bob Dylan, "This Dream of You"

They will rebuild the old ruins, raise a new city out of the wreckage...
Take the rubble left behind and make it new.

~From Isaiah 61, *The Message*

Upon departing from an aberrant group, huge chunks of one's worldview start tumbling down like shards from a melting glacier. For some, belief in the very existence of Jesus of Nazareth can begin to shake with all the rest. This was not the case with me. I did, however, have to allow myself to be dis-illusioned, in fits and starts perhaps, and not without some pain.

SOMETHING SOMEBODY STOLE

Several years ago it was discovered that I had a cancerous tumor growing in my body. The surgery to remove it lasted three times as long as the doctor had estimated. He explained to me that the reason for this was that because the tumor had gone undetected in my body for so long—blame my fear of doctors—that it had developed an extensive web of blood vessels and whatnot to sustain itself, thus greatly complicating its removal. The disillusionment process reminds me of that operation. It was painful and messy, but necessary to prepare the way for healing.

In my case, getting rid of the weird web of confusing beliefs did not lead me to the conclusion that belief itself was a delusion. When he was excising my tumor, the surgeon eventually reached healthy tissue with the scalpel. (May I just pause to say, "Thank you, Jesus!") The most delicate part of the operation was finding that border between the malignant and the healthy tissue. I believe this principle applies with spiritual surgery as well. Discerning the healthy edge where healing can begin to take place is important.

There are a great many references in scripture to the importance of foundations. Often in biblical times people would have to rebuild structures upon the ruins of a previous structure. It was especially common in oft-conquered Jerusalem. Making sure that foundation is properly prepared is a key to a strong new building. Not everyone finds it as natural as I did to begin their new life construction on the foundation of the Christian story.

There are obviously other options when it comes to worldview. Perhaps the prevailing worldview could be described as a largely unexamined life. Focus tends to be centered on the struggle to achieve material well-being. The deeper questions of meaning are generally squeezed into peripheral issues.

When spiritual and philosophical questions do force their way past the vast array of cultural distractions and into the limelight, a few general categories seem to emerge. Beginning with the Enlightenment and gaining strength up until the present, modernity has shaped a perspective that has tended to minimize religious concerns. The conviction has grown that reality is ultimately material, void of any transcendent meaning or purpose. Whatever appearance of design is found in the universe is purely accidental. Atheists often disagree among themselves as to how questions of ethics and morality play out, but they agree that these issues originate with humankind rather than any supernatural source. One of the most celebrated atheistic thinkers of the past century, Bertrand Russell, follows this line of thought through to its logical conclusion. In his essay "A Free Man's Worship" Russell discusses the tragic isolation in which most people live. His analysis concludes humanity "is the product of causes which had no prevision of the end they were achieving...Man's origin, his growth, his hopes and fears, his loves and his beliefs, are but the outcome of accidental collocations of atoms," and therefore "no fire, no heroism, no intensity of thought and feeling can preserve an individual life beyond the grave." He foresees the ultimate extinction of all of humanity's achievement in the death of the solar system, and feels that this outcome is so nearly certain that "only on the firm foundation of unyielding despair can the soul's habitation be safely built."[59]

Perhaps some find his foundation an acceptable basis upon which to build a life. Certainly some secular humanists manage to import values to lend meaning, and there are no doubt many who find ways to motivate purpose and compassion. It is hard, though, to see how one can avoid Russell's grim conclusions if reality is truly void of any transcendent grounding. His analysis simply does not jibe with my own experience of life (unless it is a particularly bad day). For that matter, it is out of sync with the vast majority of humanity for the vast majority of history. There has been a general agreement that the visible world bleeds into an invisible world that informs the visible with meaning. There is much disagreement on the particulars of this meaning, but the conviction of the existence of a transcendent dimension is widely shared. There is something more to reality than space dust and brains.

SOMETHING SOMEBODY STOLE

I've read enough now to realize that some interpreters of neuroscience and psychology offer explanations for how our perceptions of order and meaning in the universe may result from the evolving brain. Pattern recognition is a skill that lends an advantage to humans in our survival as a hunter-gatherers and agriculturalists, and even in our socialization into advanced civilizations. It is suggested that we adapted that practice to find supernatural explanations for the unexplained events in nature. These eventually became the vehicle for projections that helped prescientific humans face their disturbing consciousness of their own mortality. These projections developed into religious systems that were in turn woven into the social fabric and culturally reinforced. As science progresses, the logic goes, we outgrow our need of these primitive superstitions. This, however, seems to take us right back into the jaws of Russell's gloomy conclusion.

It just seems to me that there is something about the texture of reality that leads us to conclude that some qualities of human life simply do not feel like chemical accidents. When we encounter the breathtaking quality of beauty, the richness of human relationships, the unparalleled power of love, or the creative genius of our finest artists, thinkers, and most inspiring leaders, it just doesn't appear to be a crap shoot.

Of course, the biblical story is not the only narrative offered to explain the transcendence we intuit. Eastern religions generally share the conviction of an invisible dimension that coexists with the visible, but they tend to minimize the significance of the material realm, defining it as illusion from which we are urged to escape. In addition, they generally describe the ultimate nature of things as impersonal. If humans are the most highly developed life form we encounter on earth, and their most unique and valued quality is personhood, it strikes me as improbable that the Source of this life should be absent of personhood. When asked if he believed God was a person, C.S. Lewis replied that God was certainly not less than a person.

The three Abrahamic faiths of Judaism, Islam, and Christianity share the biblical revelation of one true and personal God as well as many overlapping insights into the invisible world. They offer an explanation for the dilemma of the essential goodness of God's creation, and the evil we encounter on our journey through it. In terms of presenting a plan of how we can best walk in harmony with our Creator, though, Jesus' offer is unique. He offers himself as the Way. If His words are to be trusted, the invitation is ultimately verifiable: "If any man will do his will, he shall know of the doctrine, whether it be of God or whether I speak of myself."[60]

This is not the place to try to unfold a thorough apologetic for following Jesus. The history of Christianity, like the history of man, is heavily littered with horrendous acts of oppression and cruelty. It is also peppered with many irrational aberrations such as those manifest in cults. There is, however, a parallel line of those who have individually, and as communities, broken through with a light divine. There are well-known saints and heroes such as Francis of Assisi, Mother Theresa, and Martin Luther King Jr., as well as numerous others from martyrs to mystics to missionaries, who though less well advertised nonetheless seemed to tread pretty closely to the footprints of the Master. It has been said that the greatest impediment to the Christian faith has been Christians. Yet it is also true that the greatest evidence on its behalf may also be Christians. The atheist Albert Camus is quoted as saying: "One should not judge a doctrine by its by-products, but through its peaks." If we are to judge Christianity by its followers, it may be wise to judge it by those who model the Jesus way most closely.

Since leaving the group I have been delighted to discover writers of great scholarship and insight who have helped reframe the whole story for me a wonderfully refreshing way. Seeing things through a new lens has greatly reduced the intellectual difficulties that the current brand of American Evangelicalism can generate. One of the difficulties of the popular version is that it has reduced the central message to a formula for escape from damnation. I've found in rereading the Gospels without that paradigm in mind, a far richer, more challenging and attractive picture emerges. This fresh approach not only enlarges my perspective but also reveals a God, as seen in Jesus, that is truly a God that I can love without reservations.

Ultimately, the decision to believe and follow is not a purely intellectual choice. Jesus never frames it that way. He speaks of conversion as a new way of believing "to see the things of the kingdom." His invitation is to come unto Him, not to simply accept a set of doctrines about Him or to confess a formulaic prayer. It is invitation to intimacy. That, indeed, may be a stumbling block to refugees from bad religion.

Intimacy requires trust. Broken trust makes trusting again so much more difficult. Heartbreak songs often express this emotion: *I am a rock, I am an island—I have no need of friendship for friendship causes pain—I'll never fall in love again.* Scripture repeatedly speaks of offense as erecting impenetrable walls. What was once open shuts tight. The promise that this time things will be different falls on deaf ears. Mark Twain observed that a cat that has once stepped on a hot stove will not step on a hot stove again. But it is also unlikely that he will ever step on a cold stove again either.

Often when God or His messengers appear to humans in the Bible they preface their revelations with a reassurance to "Fear not." When the presence of God breaks into our everyday lives, it can be more than a little disconcerting. In the wake of spiritual dislocation, the intimidation factor can be even greater. The first thing God does is to try and make us feel safe, to help us to be willing to let our guard down a little, to relax our overcharged defense mechanisms.

I do not think that we can be simply talked into trust. Jesus speaks of no one being able to come to God except drawn by the Spirit. Almost like a horse whisperer working with a traumatized animal, the Spirit has to stroke our necks and signal an absence of threat before the calming voice can do its job. Faith is a response to a Divine initiative. Perhaps most significantly, it is a gift, the gift of grace by which we are saved.

I believe that grace is the key that unlocks the door. Spiritual abuse employs heavy doses of shame to manipulate and control.

We can all vividly picture scenes where a controlling personality berates and belittles his victim until he is so broken that he visibly slumps, eyes turned inward and downward as though spun around in their sockets, defeated in spirit. He has been "dis-graced." And he—we—I need to be "re-graced."

Survivors of spiritual abuse often thirst for the message of grace. I recall an image from an old iced tea commercial: the hot, weary, pooped-out guy takes a sip his iced tea, and as he does he drops his briefcase and falls effortlessly backward into a crystal clear swimming pool, smiling and refreshed as he breathes out an utterly satisfied "A-a-a-hh!" That looks to me like the picture of the baptism of grace we all need—our insides quenched with "living water" and our outsides immersed in the "waters to swim in." "You pour out your rain in buckets, O God; thorn and cactus become an oasis for your people to camp in and enjoy."[61]

Brennan Manning, one of my favorite writers, specializes in splashing around in grace like a kid at a fire hydrant on a scorching hot day. His popular book *The Ragamuffin Gospel* has been almost a passport to Graceland for many wounded and wandering refugees from religion. I love his preface in which he points out who the book is for: "the bedraggled, beat up and burnt out ~the sorely burdened who are still shifting the heavy suitcase from one hand to the other ~the beaten and bruised who feel that their lives are a grave disappointment to God ~the inconsistent, unsteady disciples whose cheese is falling off their crackers."[62]

That was enough to get me headed for the cashier, MasterCard in hand.

In the book, Brennan quotes Robert Capon, who speaks of grace this way:

The Reformation was a time when men went blind, staggering drunk because they had discovered, in a dusty basement of late medievalism, a whole cellarful of fifteen-hundred-year-old, two-hundred-proof grace—of bottle after bottle of pure distillate of Scripture, one sip of which would convince anyone that God saves us single handedly...Grace had to be drunk straight:

SOMETHING SOMEBODY STOLE

no water, no ice, and certainly no ginger-ale, neither goodness, nor badness, nor flowers that bloom in the spring of super spirituality could be allowed to enter into the case.[63]

Set 'em up, barkeep! Like the lady said observing Meg Ryan's ecstatic outcry in the restaurant scene of *When Harry Met Sally*, "I'll take whatever she's having!"

Religion often thrives on rules and regulations, and the high-control variety that the Family frequented raised it to an art form, and a bizarre one at that. We observed strict rules about "inside" and "outside" shoes, with masking tape on the floor to demarcate where one's street shoes must stop and house slippers begin. Picture awkward, one-foot balancing acts while straddling the line to transfer feet. Yet at the same time, sexual sharing was free from "legalistic restrictions!" Please pass the camel, but hold the gnat. Ai-yai-yai!

Regardless of the variety of specific regulations, the basic deal was always to keep folks struggling to measure up to God's strict standards and "the least of these commandments," which the leaders alone were empowered to interpret. Get out the scales and make sure to get one-tenth of the spice rack tithed accurately. And let's shame those who are losing the cheese off their cracker.

When we suddenly find ourselves out of God's in-crowd, and just too exhausted to try and crawl back to the top of that elite enclave, it's mighty reassuring that there is Jesus, knocking back a cold one with the publicans and sinners, and inviting us to join them. There He stands ready to bring healing to the sick with a little transcendental medication. Like the Good Samaritan, He is stooping to pour oil and wine on the wounds of the traveler who's been robbed and beaten, and then fastidiously avoided by the priest and the Levite.

There is a fantastic picture of this kind of grace in the Oscar-winning film *Castaway*.[64] It is so packed with imagery that speaks to this journey back from spiritual shipwreck that I can only briefly touch on the highlights.

The film opens with a shot of a FedEx truck picking up a package from an attractive sculptress as she welds, listening to Elvis singing

"Heartbreak Hotel," and "All Shook Up." We soon learn that that is exactly what is in store for her, and the rest of the cast as well. The package is emblazoned with her trademark angel sculptures, which she produces and ships FedEx around the world. This one is going to her husband in Russia, who receives it while in the midst of an adulterous tryst.

While the setting is still in Moscow, the viewer is introduced to a highly efficient, self-disciplined FedEx troubleshooter named Chuck (Tom Hanks). We travel with him back to Memphis where he spends Christmas Eve with his fiancée. The dinner is suddenly interrupted by an urgent call to head back overseas. His plane crashes en route and he finds himself marooned on a deserted island. He goes through a dramatic breaking and remaking as he adapts to his new and very different surroundings. In his desperation and aloneness, he survives in part by clinging to remnants of his previous life, symbolized by a picture of his fiancée inside his broken pocket watch and one solitary unopened FedEx package—one with the emblazoned angel—which he hangs on to, maintaining a sense of purpose. Significantly, with his own blood he fashions the face of an imaginary friend/god on a Wilson volleyball that had washed ashore with him. "Wilson" seems to be all that keeps him going, and his psychological dependence upon him grows.

After a number of hopelessly feeble attempts to attract help or paddle off the heavily surf-washed island, Chuck even fails at suicide. After four years of isolation he has become a much different person. No longer a well-oiled cog in the system, he is now a primitive survivalist with a deeply superstitious dependence on Wilson. After one angry attempt at forsaking Wilson, Chuck panics and quickly repents, renewing his pledge of allegiance to him. Finally, a broken section of a port-a-potty cubicle washes ashore. After contemplating its possible usefulness, he is inspired to use is as a sail that might enable him, when the seasonal winds start to blow crosscurrent, to sail beyond the breakers and seek rescue (or death) on the open sea.

When the right conditions arise, after months of rigorous planning and preparation, he makes his break for it, paddling as far as the surf line. With a poignant glance back at the island that had become his whole frame of reference, he unfurls his sail and is up and over, out on the wide-open sea. He paddles energetically, but without any clear sense of direction, across the huge expanse, communing only with Wilson. After falling into an exhausted sleep, he suddenly awakes to the sound of a passing whale. He gazes at the behemoth that suddenly rolls to one side, revealing a mammoth eye which stares at him briefly before disappearing below the sea once again. Chuck glances quickly over at Wilson, as though to compare the wildly differing eyes of these two creations, calling to mind the huge gulf between their two creators as well.

As the voyage drags on, Chuck is suddenly awakened again to see Wilson drifting off. After a desperate attempt to retrieve Wilson, Chuck is forced to return To his badly beaten-up raft, utterly broken and weeping deep, gut-wrenching wails—first to Wilson, and then to the massive expanse of sea and sky, "I'm sorry, I'm sorry, I'm sorry..." He finally casts off his remaining oar and lies down, abandoning all of his own efforts in complete surrender. Unconscious, nearly dead, he is suddenly awakened by a massive cargo ship passing just beside him, which becomes his vehicle of rescue. The amazing grace shows up when he is finally willing to forsake his comfortable place of exile, risk the open seas, abandon the god of his own creation, and surrender his own efforts to the only power truly able to save ship-wrecked lives.

We next see Chuck back in Memphis (ironically, the home of Graceland) where he faces more shock. Not only has he been forever changed, but his entire world has, too. He learns that his fiancée has married, which forces a painful coming to terms with reality. The familiar world of FedEx, "A World of Time" as their motto goes, is no longer his home either. He behaves like a foreigner from a primitive culture, sleeping on the floor and repeatedly clicking a light on and off, a stranger in a strange land.

After a heartrending good-bye with former fiancée, Chuck sits by the fireplace of an old friend, pondering aloud the question: "What

HOW FIRM A FOUNDATION?

now? I don't know. I really don't know." He then recounts a moment of truth he'd faced on the island after his failed suicide attempt. He realized that it came down to simple plan: "Keep breathing. Because tomorrow the sun will rise. Who knows what the tide could bring?"

Following his own advice, he sets out, while listening to Elvis on the radio singing "Return to Sender," to deliver the one unopened FedEx package he'd salvaged through all of this—the last shred of purpose he still carried from his old life. After narrowly missing the sculpture-welder, as Chuck stands at the crossroads, she stops her truck to offer directions. As she pulls away, he catches a glimpse of the trademark angel wing of the back of her pickup and decides to follow the angel of welded steel.

I was taken by the string of graces that brushed Chuck's life, from the life-altering crash to the many lessons of survival, the gift of hope in the form of a sail, freedom from his self-made superstition, the rescue, the fresh hope. Grace is piled upon grace, seeing him through to a completely new life, perhaps to be welded together with another broken winged traveler.

Keep breathing. Let go of the false, and the past. Surrender to grace. Be alert for brushes with angel wings, and the new hope for what the tide may bring in.

CHAPTER 16

ANOTHER LOOK AT THE BOOK

*"Must my flock feed on what you have trampled
And drink what you have muddied with your feet?"*

~ Ezekiel 34:19

*"Ye have heard that it hath been said...
But I say unto you..."*

~ repeated by Jesus six times in Matthew 5

The Bible. Just saying the phrase out loud in a group of people can cause a deeply emotional response. Battle lines start appearing in the sand. Ammo gets pulled closer for easy reach. Some, having grown a little gun-shy, start scanning the room for the closest exit.

It really isn't hard to imagine why. For two millennia the Judeo-Christian world has struggled with this book and over this book, often using the book itself as a weapon. There are passages that describe the Word of God as a "two edged sword" and a "hammer that breaketh the rock in pieces." I have heard this quoted with odd pleasure by a theological gladiator as he defended his sport. People have both died for this book and killed for this book. Some see it as "the perfect law of liberty," others as the source of shackles for the mind and spirit. It has been used to justify slavery and to spark the movement towards abolition. It has been cited to "prove" almost every conceivable contradictory doctrine, but also has been seen as a guide that points beyond doctrine. In society at large the Bible is a hot potato. Among alumni of high-control groups it can be downright radioactive!

One of the tragedies of spiritual abuse is the use of scripture twisting. I love Jesus' remarks to the religious leaders who were locking away the liberating power of God's Word from those they were oppressing: "Woe unto you! For you have taken away the key of knowledge: ye entered not in yourselves, and them that were entering ye hindered."[65] Twisted scriptures "turned the truth of God into a lie," and in doing so have created large numbers of people with serious allergies to the Bible.

I realize that I am not completely impartial in this matter. The Bible in all its richness and wonder is no doubt one of the most powerful attractions that the Family held for me. I loved the poetic language—we were "KJV only," of course. Its stories were a source of fascination. I was intrigues by the strange tales of a tribe of people interacting with this all-powerful and mysterious Yahweh. This Voice thundering from the cloud-covered mountaintop at times seemed poised to hurl lightning bolts, while at others the Lord was drawn to the sweet melodies from a young shepherd's harp. And this tribe of Hebrews was a whole 'nuther story. What a cast of characters. Talk about dysfunctional families!

At the center of whole shebang is Jesus. Reading the stories of His radical countercultural behavior and turn-the-world-on-its-head parables was always a doorway to another dimension for me. And the stuff His early followers experienced and wrote about seemed to re-root me in an entirely different realm.

But before I get too carried away, as time went on in the movement, the flipside of scripture was popping up with increasing frequency and with greater volume and distortion. The Bible was becoming the source of gradually more bizarre destructive practices. It became a tool of control, used to keep us from the "dangers" of doubt, murmuring, and the most lethal of all, rebellion. So it is not surprising that for many, the Bible can trigger a strongly negative, even visceral response. If the Bible is misused as a tool of control in a systematic and prolonged way, the "fight or flight" response is more or less to be expected in at least some of it's victims.

My personal relationship to scripture developed somewhat differently than it did for many of my fellow travelers. From day one the book took on a life of its own for me. It was not simply the Yellow Pages in which to locate "proof texts" to support various doctrines. It held an almost magical quality for me. I could lose myself in its pages. At times I would be reading, and it felt like I could almost hear Paul's voice or be standing among the crowds as Jesus taught and healed. The heart cry of the psalmists would resonate in my inner being, "deep calling unto deep," unleashing hot tears of repentance and longing. I found even the rhythm of the words read aloud could alter my state of consciousness.

Of course, I also had my times of saving up "proof texts." In leadership, parenting, and even marriage I found some passages very useful in (ahem...) clarifying questions of authority. I also had my fair share of experiences of getting bopped on the bean with the Bible. But by and large, I was in love with this collection of ancient texts and could recount numerous experiences of God's Promises being fulfilled in my own life.

When things began to come unraveled in my cultic worldview, and the ground underneath my feet began to shift, I turned back to the Bible. I had somehow kept the habit, long since abandoned as official policy, of working out some scriptural support for even the bizarre stuff coming down the pipeline. My biblical theology was getting more like "Picasso meets Tinker Toys" all the time, but the habit eventually saved me. As I recounted earlier, when I could no longer make this crazy hodgepodge of Family beliefs stand up, it was the Bible that once again became my guide to sift through the confusion. And it was the Bible that picked me up and carried me out of the grip of the group.

For a number of years after leaving, it remained a top priority for me to try and discover the unspoiled terrain of "correct doctrine." I searched on for that place that could be the foundation upon which to rebuild, like a pilgrim in the New World. Alas, it came as a difficult awakening to realize that this land of doctrinal correctness was about as elusive as the home of "Puff the Magic Dragon." We will always be pilgriming on, always subject to shifts in the tectonic plates of our human understanding, and to some extent "squinting through the fog,"[66] as St. Paul puts it. Eventually I learned to be comfortable in the pilgrim mode.

It is interesting to observe the different ways refugees from abusive groups cope with the journey forward and the Bible's place in their trek. There is a certain segment that deals with the issue by simply replacing the group's authoritarian, if unorthodox, view of scripture, with a new and equally unquestioning allegiance to a strict fundamentalist and rigidly orthodox reading. One can understand the comfort of having clear-cut, absolute certainty, especially when this comes with the social reinforcement of a large population of loyal adherents. It not only acts as a powerful bulwark against the logic of the aberrant group you have left behind, but also locates you in a new identity and safe subculture to equip you to survive in a world coming unglued by its conflicting worldviews.

I found this approach ultimately unsatisfying. It started to become more and more obvious to me that there was no possible way to get the entire package of doctrinal Lego blocks to all snap together neatly. Even close theological neighbors seemed to have very different ways of reading the book and of settling the many questions it raised. Just when I thought I had one section of the wall neat and complete, a block would pop out somewhere else. And when I tried to push that one block in, two from the first section popped back out. Each answer seemed to generate two more questions, and all attempts to square the circle started to feel more and more like the intellectual dishonesty and cognitive dissonance of group life. I still managed to hold certain key elements solidly in my center of vision, but was having to let go of more and more issues blurring out in my peripherals. "Oh yeah," I recalled, "through a glass darkly."

But then what to do with the Bible? The good ol' B-I-B-L-E, that's the book for me, I stand alone on the cornerstone, amen brother, Bible. The picture of writers from Moses on down, sitting at a table, taking word-for-word dictation from God, who carefully edited for typos and misunderstandings, simply did not jibe with what even conservative scholars had to say about the Bible's arrival on earth. This was a collection of documents from a wide variety of sources, many times unknown sources, that included history, poetry, collections of wise sayings, imaginative tales, liturgies and letters, songs of love and lament. In places it read more like *Pirates of the Caribbean* than a systematic theology. If we are to take the Bible primarily as a source book for religious rules and rituals, we'd have to admit it appears to have been poorly planned. And yet, it clearly told a story of a unique and continually unfolding relationship between God and His creatures. I find an elegant logic in the narrative as it builds to its climax in Jesus and His impact upon the planet. It wasn't as clear as the "just follow the instructions" version that the Family and other parts of the religious community point to with pride, but it was compelling. Messy perhaps, but alive, and full of power to give meaning and bring a sense of connection to the Big Story.

Serendipitously, I started to stumble upon authors who seemed to have words to help me think about the scriptures in a new, and more life-giving way.[67] I came across a passage in an interview in which Fredrick Buechner paraphrases the theologian Karl Barth:

He says that reading the Bible is like looking down from a building onto the street and seeing everyone looking up, pointing to something. Because of the way the window is situated you can't see what they're seeing but you realize they are seeing something of extraordinary importance. That is what it is like to read the Bible. It is full of people, all pointing up at some extraordinary event. All those different fingers are pointing at truths, all those different voices are babbling about truth in all the Bible's different forms...it has to do basically with the presence of God in history...it is a living truth in the sense that it is better experienced than explained.[68]

Of course, this sort of talk is likely to make some people a little jittery, but I have been pleasantly surprised to find an amazing number of serious students of the Word who, rather than using this inexactness as an excuse to blow the whole thing off, actually let the mystery draw them into a deeper commitment to engage the text. They wrestle with scripture like Jacob with the angel, letting it pull them into the story more powerfully and refusing to let go without the blessing. If we approach the Bible with the idea that it lays out in clarity and unambiguous detail an exhaustive picture of the infinite God and comprehensive view of all that ever was, is, or shall be, then we are surely setting ourselves up for disappointment. On the other hand, seeing the story as an expression of the ongoing relationship between the mysterious and infinite God and His extremely finite people, a story that continues to shed light on His current dealings with us as well as point the way towards its final destination, then it comes alive in a way that is more relational than merely informational.

There is a fascinating story in II Kings 22. After a generation of corrupt and destructive rule under King Manasseh, a young teenager named Josiah comes to the throne. He is determined to clean up the mess and get Israel back to the blessing they'd enjoyed when they had been in close fellowship with the Creator. The Temple had fallen into ruin through years of neglect, so Josiah hires some honest and skilled folks to restore it to useful condition. During the project a priest and a scribe uncover "The Book of the Law" in the mess. Once recovered from the rubble, it becomes a road map to renewal in the land. It seems that every so often we need to do that with the Bible—shovel off layers of debris and take a fresh look with new eyes.

I have grown annoyed with the expression *"The Bible says..."* as an unassailable proof that whatever follows is "the Word of God."

ANOTHER LOOK AT THE BOOK

Heck, the Bible says, *"There is no God."* (Psalm 14:1—*"The fool hath said in his heart 'There is no God.'"*) Whatever is being quoted must be kept in the context of the passage, and then thoughtfully approached before applying it to a specific situation. Otherwise, you'll get snake handlers quoting Mark 16:18 to justify their practices, and stuff like David Berg's reworking of the New Testament principle of the law of love to justify all manner of sexual meanderings. Contrary to the "preconceived notion" or "isn't that convenient" schools of interpretation that prevails in some circles, I've found it very helpful to read a little more on the historical background of different portions of scripture, and try to make sense of what is going on. Who is speaking? Are they inspired and speaking for God, or representing another point of view? (For example, the Psalms, Job, and Ecclesiastes, all include material from various points of view.) I've come to the conclusion that interpretation is not always an exact science. In fact, there seems to be a blend of art and science.

In addition to sorting out context and meaning, there is the additional challenge of trying to ascertain the application of a passage in one's present circumstances. In his recent book *The Blue Parakeet— Rethinking How You Read the Bible*,[69] biblical scholar and author Scot McKnight highlights the ways in which all readers of scripture are forced to discern how a particular passage ought to be applied. He goes to great lengths to help readers keep in mind the overarching story as they engage each particular text. He also explains the nature of revelation in human language through human authors and the very human ways we interact with God. He quickly debunks the approach Of "God said it, I believe it, and that settles it!" The idea behind this saying is that we believe everything the Bible says and therefore practice whatever it says. He points out that no congregation he knows of practices all of the Bible's directives. Examples range from strict biblical observance of Sabbath prohibitions to dietary restrictions, rules concerning dress, haircuts, beards, and stoning young people who show disrespect to elders, just to name a few. New Testament examples also abound. Clearly everyone applies some standard of picking and choosing to discern what applies today, and how to best apply it. The huge variety of interpretations of how we are to pick, choose, and apply is witnessed in the wide variety of denominations and their distinctives. So apparently that does not "settle it," despite what the bumper-sticker claims. McKnight's book does an excellent job of challenging readers to think through the "patterns of discernment" we see throughout scripture and church history, while constantly reminding us of the importance of reading relationally.

Again, Jesus is the center of it all. He told the religious scholars of His day something surprising: "You have heads in your Bibles constantly because you think you'll find eternal life in there. But you miss the forest for the trees. These scriptures are all about me! And I am here, standing right now in front of you, and you aren't willing to receive from me the life you say you want."[70] It's not just about learning stuff—it's about knowing Him.

I believe in careful study and exegesis, learning historical context, and consulting commentaries on original language and customs. Thoughtful discussions can be very helpful to enlarge our understandings and so on. But, I came upon this passage in a little book with the great title *Reading the Bible for the Love of God*. I thought it expressed the key idea beautifully:

Entering the Bible on its own terms requires that we read it in a way that is radically different from the way we read most other books, and perhaps, radically different from what we have traditionally thought of Bible reading. When we read the Bible for the facts alone, our hearts tend to be deadened to the Word of God. When we read it for the who, instead of the what, we may begin to take on a bit of the radiance of the love of God.[71]

That approach would certainly be more helpful to most of us than trying to puzzle things out through a sort of "cut and paste" technique. It might actually become the "lamp unto our feet" that we seek as we continue down the road.

CHAPTER 17

THIS IS YOUR BRAIN ON PAIN

Canst thou not minister to a mind disease'd:
Pluck from the memory a rooted sorrow,
Raze out the written troubles of the brain;
And, with some sweet oblivious antidote,
Cleanse the stuff'd bosom of that perilous stuff,
Which weighs upon the heart?

~ Shakespeare, *Macbeth*, Act v, Scene 3

In looking at the spiritual and psychological impact of abuse and the challenges one encounters on the road to recovery, sooner or later one is bound to stumble on another matter: the "gray matter." It turns out that when something messes with your head it quite literally messes with your head. Researchers have found in recent years that abuse and psychological trauma can affect the actual architecture of the brain and dramatically impact its ability to function. The recovery program at Meadowhaven began several years ago to address this issue.

In the world of cult recovery one often comes across the term Post Traumatic Stress Disorder, or PTSD. PTSD has been in the news quite a lot recently in the coverage surrounding the psychological challenges faced by soldiers returning from Iraq and Afghanistan. It is described as an anxiety disorder that can develop after exposure to one or more traumatic events producing an ongoing emotional reaction. It manifests in a group of symptoms often seen to varying degrees in some cult survivors. The symptoms can include flashbacks or nightmares, avoidance of stimuli (or "triggers") associated with the traumatic experience, difficulty sleeping, anger, and hyper vigilance. It is believed to stem from an overload of the "fight or flight" reaction to intense or prolonged stress, and the neurochemical imbalance that can result from it.

In my conversations with Bob and Judy about the Meadowhaven program, the topic of trauma and its continuing effect on residents seemed to come up quite often. When I expressed a desire to learn more about the subject they suggested reading *Trauma and Recovery* by Judith Herman. Published in 1992, this landmark study examines the controversial history of the term "trauma" as it is applied to victims of violence ranging from domestic abuse to political terror. I was surprised to learn that the term has only fairly recently come to be understood in its psychological sense.

The first time the issue surfaced was in late nineteenth century France. Its focus was in relation to the work of a pioneering French neurologist, Jean-Martin Charcot, working in a French asylum caring for beggars, prostitutes, and the insane. In his interviews with many of the women who had led lives of constant abuse and exploitation, Charcot was the first to lend credibility to women suffering from what at the time was called "hysteria." This was a term for a psychological ailment thought unique to women and actually thought to originate in the uterus, hence, the term "hysteria." Until Charcot began his studies, victims of hysteria were regarded as malingerers, without any serious attempt to treat them. Although I found accounts of his case studies rather bizarre by modern sensibilities, he is credited with developing a diagnosis of symptoms and exploring the earliest attempts at treatment of psychological trauma.

Charcot's studies were followed by attempts by Sigmund Freud and Pierre Janet to explore the causes of hysteria. By the mid 1890s, hysteria had been linked to psychological trauma producing an altered state of consciousness known as "dissociation." Janet believed dissociation to be a sign of psychological weakness and suggestibility, while Freud and his colleague Joseph Breuer argued that it could be found among "people of the clearest intellect, strongest well, greatest character, and the highest critical power." [72]

In the midst of ensuing debates on all things related to hysteria, Freud eventually concluded that hysteria was often linked to sexual abuse, including rape and incest, often during childhood. However, the malady was so widespread, even among the respectable classes, that at the time the implication of perversion on such a scale was considered unthinkable. Eventually, he was forced to retract his theory and began to attribute the causes of traumatic dissociation to the erotic fantasies of the victims. The whole topic was eventually dropped like a hot potato and avoided for years. Those who suffered from the condition were once again forgotten.

The issue of psychological trauma again surfaced in a very different context during the First World War. In four years over eight million men died in horrific conditions. In the midst of the slaughter and devastation many soldiers began to exhibit symptoms similar to those of "hysterical" women. The nervous disorder was soon labeled "shell shock." It became so prevalent that it has been estimated that mental breakdowns accounted for 40 percent of British casualties.

The traditionalist view of the condition linked it to cowardice and shirking, and advocated shaming, punishments, and even electric shock for treatment. More progressive views saw it as unrelated to moral character and advocated a more humane treatment based on the principles of psychoanalysis. In one of the most famous cases involving a highly decorated war hero, the treatment was deemed a success because they had persuaded him to recant his antiwar position and return to battle, motivated by his love for his fellow soldiers. Although some fresh insights were gained, the connection to hysteria was not examined. After the war the public was only too happy to forget the whole thing, ignoring the many veterans left to languish in asylums long after the armistice.

World War II revived medical interest in combat neurosis. It was eventually recognized that any man could break down under sustained, severe combat conditions. Experiments with hypnosis and sodium amytol did not relieve the condition. Most suffers were simply returned to some kind of duty within a week, often to combat. At the war's end, interest once again waned.

The next chapter begins in the aftermath of the Vietnam War. Robert Jay Lifton, of Thought Reform fame, and a colleague began meeting with Vietnam veterans. The vets questioned the popular image of the socialized warrior and the justification for the war. Antiwar "rap sessions" became arenas where vets retold and relived their traumatic war experiences among themselves. What subsequently emerged was a clear delineation of "Post Traumatic Stress Disorder." By 1980 it became a recognized diagnosis.

At the same time on a parallel track, the women's movement was exploring issues related to the exploitation of women. This triggered a great deal of fresh research on sexual assault. The implication of widespread abuse in society at large that had caused Freud to back off his initial linkage with "hysteria" to childhood trauma was in fact true. The statistics were, and are, horrifying.

Eventually the connection was drawn between the post-traumatic stress disorder of the Vietnam vets and the psychological trauma of women who were victims of sexual assault, childhood abuse, and/or domestic violence. The symptoms pointed to the same basic trauma of the mind.

The connection to the trauma of abuse within the cultic environment, often with a strong sexual and high-control element, was obvious. The most shocking example of this traumatic abuse within the Family was with Merry Berg, David Berg's own granddaughter. Merry had been largely raised by Jane Berg, David Berg's first wife, in a highly disorganized fashion, with an atmosphere of super-spirituality and magical thinking rare even by Family standards. When she was a young preteen, Merry and another preteen girl were brought to live in her grandfather's home. She was not only exposed to a great deal of sexual abuse perpetrated by her grandfather—often while he was drunk—but was also constantly subjected to obsessive scrutiny of her thought life, searching for any signs of doubt or disloyalty. She was alternately praised and berated, and when she finally uttered a criticism of Berg she was subjected to an incredible barrage of violent punishments, scathing rebukes, and bizarre exorcisms, sometimes while actually tied to her bed. On top of all that, Berg had the sessions transcribed and published for the Family's "edification," as a sort of template for how to deal with young people who opened themselves to "demonic doubts." Although I never witnessed anything quite that extreme, the general spirit of the approach did spread to many areas of the world, being incorporated into the teen training philosophy. I still recall being in London when we received the account entitled "The Last State"—a reference to Jesus' tale of a demoniac who after deliverance again invites possession and "his last state was worse than the first." I was already growing deeply suspicious of the spirit at work in the movement. This was one more straw breaking my camel's back. Merry and many others who received this medieval treatment have struggled with the devastating impact of this abuse for decades.

It took me awhile to recognize symptoms in my own life, but eventually I noticed a pattern of behavior that related to authority issues. Berg's NPD mood swings affected every level of authority within the Family, leaving us continually off balance. There would be periods of liberalization when an innovative spirit was lauded and pioneers were encouraged to launch new ministries. Music groups, radio and television outreaches, and even entrepreneurial ventures would blossom. Then, without warning, the wind would shift with the suddenness of a Maoist cultural revolution, when strict conformity and blind obedience would be the only values of importance, quickly quenching individual initiative and getting us to immediately clam up and just try to avoid the attention of any "off with their heads!" directives headed our way. Similarly, lenient shepherding styles might enjoy favor for a period, but these would be swallowed overnight by a letter such as "God Hates Murmuring!" which might have been triggered by a casual comment Berg took as a criticism, causing him to go ballistic and the entire leadership structure to go hard line. I caught serious flack a number of times, including highly emotional "disciplines" such as having mates and children relocated and so on. Decades of this had me burying casks full of 100-proof Irish temper deep in my spirit. Long after having left the group and well into a new career, I eventually ended up in somewhat of a leadership role in an independent sales force. Corporate might issue a new policy that I did not feel properly considered the concerns of the field, and all of a sudden my blood pressure would skyrocket and my face turn red, just before I'd erupt with, shall we say, a less than diplomatic approach to problem solving. Oops. Eventually I made the connection and realized that a lot of this emotion was cult hangover. That knowledge has helped me recognize and rope off danger spots, and eventually try to defuse them like leftover mines from a long-forgotten war.

Stephanie's triggers were often related to the kids. In the Family, there were always threats to the stability of your parent/child relationship. Parents were not the ultimate authority in a child's upbringing. To slightly misquote the axiom: "It takes a cult to raise a child." This carried over into her somewhat obsessive hovering over the children, partly as a protective instinct and partly as a self-protective one. Events that have happened after we left the group have led to re-traumatization as well. It is only after decades of struggle that Stephanie has come to recognize these forces and really seek help to overcome what can be a debilitating fear. And we were adults when this stuff happened.

I have to confess that spending a concentrated amount of time trying to get a handle on the issue of trauma was deeply unsettling. Realizing the extent to which this abuse, especially of young minds, actually altered neurological development left me pretty despondent.

Shaken, I asked Bob for something I might read that could offer any hope. He suggested two books: *The Brain That Changes Itself* by Norman Doidge, MD, and *The Boy Who Was Raised as a Dog* by Bruce D. Percy, MD, PhD, and Maia Szalavitz.

The Brain That Changes Itself is an introduction to the fascinating world of neuroplasticity. Doidge examines how thoughts can change the structure and function of the brain, which remains amazingly plastic even into old age. He presents to the reader a series of brilliant scientists exploring neuroplasticity and recounts some almost unbelievable stories of people whose lives have been transformed by discoveries in the field. The publisher's blurb on the book jacket summarizes *"...introducing principles we can all use as well as a riveting collection of case histories—stroke patients cured, a woman with half a brain that rewired itself to function as a whole, learning and emotional disorders overcome, IQs raised, and aging brains rejuvenated..."*[73] These stories are, well, "mind-bending," and deeply, deeply inspiring. The concept lends hope that the impact of intense psychological trauma on the physical architecture of the brain can be overcome.

The most upsetting thing for me was the understanding that trauma's strongest impact occurs in childhood, because this is when the brain is in its most formative stages. Thinking about what some of the kids raised in the Family went through and observing their struggles later in life can be difficult and disheartening. The second title Bob had recommended was particularly helpful in dealing with this issue. *The Boy Who Was Raised as a Dog*[74] recounts stories from Dr. Bruce Perry's work with troubled children. Over the last few decades he has treated children traumatized by unimaginable horror: genocide survivors, witnesses to their own parents' murders, children raised in closets and cages, and especially relevant, the Branch Davidian children who survived Waco. Perry clearly explains what happens to a child's brain when exposed to extreme stress. As he talks about each child and the unique problems he or she presented, we see him challenge the status quo understanding of child psychiatry and the way it was too often practiced. He shares how he came to fresh insights and innovative methods for helping to ease the pain of these children and allowing them to develop into healthy adults. The stories often read like a mystery, as Bruce uncovers the science of the mind at work in these children and puts together intuitive treatments that bring hope and healing to the spirit of even the most wounded child. One experience builds upon another, as we see how patience, understanding, and love manage to break through what seems to be insurmountable walls.

These two books share a view of the brain that has been severely impacted by trauma and abuse that when combined, offer the possibility of healing. At Meadowhaven, Bob and Judy began several years ago to work with residents whose experience had impacted some of the cognitive functions of the brain. While watching a PBS Special dealing with brain plasticity, they began to realize that a "Brain Fitness Program" developed by Posit Science to help aging people keep their brains functioning at a high level seemed to address some of the challenges faced by those recovering from the trauma of abuse as well. They ordered the program and have gotten very encouraging results. A number of residents increased their scores on cognitive tests significantly. The program was developed by California scientific Michael Merzenich, the brain behind Posit Science. Merzenich's work is discussed at length in chapter three of Doidge's book. Bob and Judy have discussed their experience with the developers of the program, and it does seem as though the needs of the traumatized brain have a significant overlap with those of the aging brain. This is especially good news to those of us who are *both* traumatized and aging! Although much more remains to be learned in connection to the brain, there is room for much hope.

There are a number of other evidence-based practices that have proven helpful to trauma survivors such as cognitive behavioral therapy, art therapy, EMDR (Eye Movement Desensitization and Reprogramming), Mindfulness Meditation, The National Institute for Traumatic Loss in Children, and many more resources on the Internet. There are also a number of effective, specifically Christian approaches to spiritual healing, for those open to that option. (I touch on this later.)

One major challenge to healing through any of the avenues is the natural resistance to psychological treatments of any type that can exist in cult survivors. Cultic beliefs often instill barriers of fear and distrust of psychology and psychological therapies. In addition, trauma survivors often develop elaborate defense mechanisms that can make it difficult to accept help of this kind. Highly defended people do not change easily, as letting down their guard is tantamount to opening themselves up to further injury. It is a catch-22. Bob and Judy compare the process of avoidance to living in a large house, but closing off the doors—one by one—to any rooms where the trauma victim experiences discomforting triggers. Eventually they find themselves restricted to life in a tiny corner of the house. If that situation becomes unbearable they may finally seek help to unlock those doors and find their way back to a fuller experience of life, one full of renewed hope, rather than accepting the confinement of settling down with hopelessness.

A lot of research into brain function is currently pursuing links between neuroscience and spirituality. One book I've recently been reading with great interest is *How God Changes Your Brain* by Andrew Newberg, MD, and Mark Robert Waldman,[75] a research team at the Center for Spirituality and the Mind at the University of Pennsylvania. Without taking any position on specific religious traditions, this team examines the latest research concerning the neurological impact of various religious and relaxation practices. They cull evidence from brain scan studies and numerous surveys to draw conclusions about how taking positive practical steps can make your brain and life better. They find that not only can prayer and spiritual practice reduce stress and anxiety, but just twelve minutes a day of meditation may slow down the aging process. They conclude that contemplating a loving God rather than a punitive God reduces anxiety, depression, and stress, and increases feelings of security, compassion, and love. They point out that religious belief in itself is benign and can be personally beneficial, but anger, fear, and prejudice sometimes generated by extreme beliefs can permanently damage the brain. On the other hand, religious practices of prayer and meditation can positively change numerous structures and functions in the brain.

One particularly relevant insight I drew from the book is that the human brain has developed in such a way as to have a prejudice for negative information. It is fairly easy to see why alarm bells triggering the fight-or-flight response can prove more critical to survival than recognizing positive opportunities. Avoiding a predator is more urgent than discovering a possible new resource. This causes us to give heavier psychological weight the negative factors in our environment. These circuits tend to make it harder to shake a negative thought pattern, which underlines the dangers of constantly replaying negative memories. It was very interesting to note that when we constantly pull out memories and rehearse them, they get re-filed with an even darker tinge and stronger negative emotion, especially if they are shared in an atmosphere of other reinforcing negative voices. There can be a downside to venting, if we aren't careful.

Newberg and Waldman offer a number of strategies to help us become more aware of our self-defeating mental processes and develop healthier outlooks and emotions. These range from simple breathing exercises that alter stress levels to relaxation techniques, meditation and centering prayer, walking meditation, tracking our own thought processes, and consciously directing ourselves to positive thoughts and emotions. (Even yawning! You gotta read it!) They also bring out the influence of music, media, and surroundings, and the importance of good nutritional and exercise habits.

From a more specifically spiritual perspective, my wife and I have drawn great encouragement from a very simple book written more than a half a century ago by one of the pioneers of the modern healing movement, Agnes Sanford. In her classic *The Healing Light*,[76] Sanford relates experiences from her own spiritual journey, including deep battles with depression. She boils the subject matter down to some very simple principles that can be accessed even by those who are uncertain of their beliefs about God. Stephanie and I have drawn tremendous comfort and reassurance from her insights in our personal struggles with discouragement, depression, and grief. Sanford helps us to recognize that God's light is constantly surrounding us, and His healing energy is accessed through the childlike trust. The exercise of visualizing God's power working in us to gently heal us can provide some amazing results. When I read Sanford I feel as though I am being quietly ushered into an atmosphere of faith and helped to tap into the warm creative energy of God's healing presence. Some approaches to faith and healing can be overly hyped and put unhelpful pressure on the one seeking healing, or condemn those whose faith is struggling. I am reminded of the honest response of the father of the oppressed child when Jesus had drawn a connection between faith and healing. The father cries out, "Lord, I believe. Help thou my unbelief." If we open ourselves in this way, admitting that our faith is imperfect, God honors our approach.

Personally, I recognize that sometimes I hesitate at the invitation to healing. There is a classic scene in the Gospels when Jesus comes upon a man, who has been paralyzed for thirty-eight years, waiting at a pool reputed to offer healing to those who bathed in its waters at special times. He has been unable to get in on it, not having anyone to help him in "at the troubling of the waters." Jesus asks him a question that seems heavy with implications: "Do you want to be healed?" Seems like kind of a dumb question. What else would he be hanging at the side of the pool for? But the question really seems aimed at all of us—do we really want to risk letting go of our identity as sufferers, even if the identity is paralyzing us? If invited to take up our bed and walk, will we take a chance, even if we fear that it might lead to us falling down again? Jesus puts the ball in our court. I don't think it is always easy, but I believe if we allow ourselves to imagine a positive outcome and a paralysis-free life, it will seem worth it to give trust one more try.

It is not very difficult to see how all these aspects of the human make-up—body, mind, and spirit—are part of the healing process. And there is reason for great hope for wholeness and health in all. "Therefore my heart is glad, and my soul rejoices: my body also rests secure" (Psalm16:9).

CHAPTER 18

THE F WORD

I've been tryin' to get down
To the heart of the matter
But my will gets weak
And my thoughts seem to scatter
But I think it's about…
Forgiveness…

~ Don Henley "Heart of the Matter"

If there is one hot button sure to raise an uproar in discussions among ex-members, it is broaching the subject of forgiveness. After stumbling onto this hornet's nest a few times, I began to realize that there had to be something I was missing, and I began trying to better understand this emotional response. It was perceived as an insensitive slap in the face to imply in any way that folks who had been victimized, or whose children had been victimized, might in some way benefit from a renewed understanding of forgiveness. But wait, please, before slamming the book closed and jumping on the Internet to shred me, let me try to explain.

In reading up on the subject I learned that it is quite common for victims of abuse or of various crimes to react angrily to any hint that forgiveness may in some way be a step toward their healing. After all, they were the victims, for cryin' out loud! Why the heck should they have to forgive? Especially when the doggone perps won't even acknowledge the truth of what happened, much less repent, or sincerely ask for forgiveness! Sheesh. Give us a friggin' break! Revenge is a subject that might be a little easier to warm up to. That concept offers, at least, some way of regaining control, of evening the score, of writing a new ending to the story. Anger can provide some measure of comfort, at least as a way to refocus the pain. Who can't relate to that?

Initially, the concept I had of forgiveness stemmed largely from a religious point of view. It was something that I thought of simply as a duty to a biblical injunction, and I never really pondered much as to why it should be so. After getting a taste of the anger that raising the concept could unleash, I began to read through some of the literature on the subject from a therapeutic perspective rather than a purely religious one.

I was surprised to learn that the question of forgiveness had been pretty much ignored in the literature of the therapeutic community until fairly recently. In the early eighties Dr. Mack Harnden went to the library of the University of Kansas to look up the word *forgiveness* in the Psychological Abstracts and found no entries at all.[77]

At roughly the same time Robert Enright, a professor at the University of Wisconsin, was searching for a research project in the field of moral development that could have a genuine impact on society. "I kept asking myself, 'If the social sciences are supposed to be part of the helping professions, and if the wisdom of the ages—the Hebrew-Christian Bible—is replete with wonderful stories of the success of person-to-person forgiveness, why haven't the social sciences even thought to study forgiveness as a primary investigation?'"[78] Nearly a decade passed while the grant committees shunned his proposals and yielded not a single dollar for research.

At long last, Enright's work came to public attention via a story in *The Chicago Tribune*. The public response was overwhelming!

Finally the spigot of research money was opened, and Enright's International Forgiveness Institute shot to the forefront of forgiveness research. Many other academic institutions have joined the quest with projects being funded for researching the impact that forgiveness has on numerous areas of human suffering. Jimmy Carter, Archbishop Desmond Tutu, and Elizabeth Elliot, a former missionary who led a mission team back into the jungle to reach out to the very tribe of headhunters who had killed her husband, are now leading a ten-million-dollar campaign for forgiveness research with a global political focus.

Both Dr. Harnden and Professor Enright credit one source for having helped focus their research and the world's attention on the issue: theologian Lewis Smedes and his landmark 1983 book, *Forgive and Forget*. Harnden says of Smedes's impact that his message "directed the course of my life, because I felt that forgiveness is the core, [the] most significant factor in both spiritual and psychological healing."[79] Smedes found that in the past "human forgiveness had been seen as a religious obligation of love, the love we owe to the person who offended us. The discovery that I made was the important benefit that forgiving is to the forgiver. And this is where I think the link between the psychological research and my book is."[80]

Stumbling upon this insight provided me with a personal "Aha!" moment. It became completely understandable why an injured party would be triggered to anger by any suggestion of an obligation to forgive the wrongdoer. However, the point of forgiveness is primarily to benefit the victim. As Smedes points out: "To forgive is to set a prisoner free, and discover that prisoner was you!"[81]

Smedes speaks movingly of the work of Jewish philosopher Hannah Arendt, who had been an eyewitness to the trial of Adolf Eichman. In her book, *The Human Condition*, Arendt observes, "The only remedy for the inevitability of history is forgiveness." Smedes comments, "She means that in the natural course of things we are stuck with our past and its effects on us. We may forget our history, but we cannot undo it. One thing only can release us from the grip of our history. That one thing is forgiveness."[82]

I think it is important, in the effort to find a renewed understanding of forgiveness, to quickly clarify what forgiveness is *not*:

FORGIVENESS IS NOT EXCUSING. Forgiving can only happen when we refuse to excuse.

FORGIVENESS IS NOT SMOOTHING THINGS OVER. Smoothing things over, like a mother or a manager, prevents forgiving because it stifles hurt. It took me awhile to let this point to sink in. Forgiving only happens when we first admit our hurts, and scream our rage. In the Family and other groups like it, when a mistake was made that was so egregious that it couldn't be completely covered up, an injured party was often urged to a quick forgiveness. The idea is to perhaps show a little sympathy to the injured, demonstrating the compassion of leadership, and get the plaintiff's emotions on their side, and then lean on the victim's sense of Christian duty to do the right thing, to be magnanimous, "Christ-like," and of course to put the greater good and unity first by forgiving. Leadership might throw in a little slap on the wrist to the offender, say a quick prayer, and "Praise the Lord, isn't it good to get all that behind us." No fuss, no muss. The Revolution marches on. In their dealings with ex-members, Family Leadership is almost legendary for their insincere attempts to elicit forgiveness from those who have been hurt by their policies. Beginning with the onset of high-profile court cases and negative publicity in the nineties, it seemed like every year or two they would issue some official apology to former members, especially those of the second generation who had clearly suffered the most. It was sort of a little "Whoopsey-daisey, so sorry about that. We didn't mean to hurt anyone, somebody must have misunderstood, and apparently mistakes were made. Please forgive us. Okey-dokey. All better now." If the fountains of forgiveness did not flow forth freely they were a little surprised, but they soon came to define the problem as stemming from the bitterness in the hearts of the unforgiving ex-members springing up to defile many.

Dr. Harnden points out along these lines: "Forgiveness does not preclude the enforcement of healthy and natural consequences on the offender...Whenever an individual offends another, the offender gives up a certain degree of power in determining his or her own destiny, with the power being given over to the offended."[83]

Smedes again: "Some people view forgiveness as a cheap avoidance of justice, a plastering over of the wrong. A sentimental make-believe. If forgiveness is a whitewashing of wrong, then it itself is wrong. Nothing that whitewashes evil can be good. It can be good only if it is a redemption from the effects of evil, not a make-believing that evil never happened."[84]

With these principles in mind, perhaps forgiveness will lose some of its powerful distastefulness in the eyes of rightfully angry individuals. It is *not* a religious obligation towards the offender, but rather a step on the path to healing for the *victim*, a leg on his or her own journey *out* of the pain. It still may not feel very fair, but Smedes asks,

Is it fair to be stuck to a painful past? Is it fair to be walloped again and again by the old unfair hurt? Vengeance is having a videotape planted in your soul that cannot be turned off. It plays the painful scene over and over again inside your mind. It hooks you into its instant replays. And each time it replays, you feel the clap of pain again. Is this fair? Forgiving turns off the videotape. [85]

But how? After admitting that it is something we cannot do but sometimes do anyway, Smedes shares three things he noticed about how people forgive. I summarize:

<u>They forgive slowly</u>. C.S. Lewis had a sadistic teacher when he was a boy that he hated for most of his life. Late in his life he wrote to a friend: "Do you know; only a few weeks ago I realized suddenly that I had at last forgiven the cruel schoolmaster who had so darkened my childhood. I had been trying to do it for years."[86]

Essentially, we cannot; but eventually, we do. It doesn't usually happen all at once. Sometimes it just takes a commitment to begin the process. Once we begin to become aware of the unhealthy ways anger and rage can eat away at our insides (sometimes literally!) we can learn to recognize our response to triggers as they arise and consciously choose to refuse to jump in. Change channels. Pass on the past and tune into the present, while building a new future. Lily Tomlin quipped "To forgive is to give up all hope of a better past." If others have damaged our past, there is no reason to let them ruin our future as well.

<u>They forgive communally</u>. We need people who hurt as much as we hurt and who hate as much as we hate. We need people who are struggling as hard as we need to struggle before we come through with forgivingness in a fellowship of slow forgivers.[87]

After leaving, we appreciated having the benefit of close friends who traveled the same path and who shared the need to vent from time to time. Eventually we just sort of had said it all. It became obvious to us that it was time to let it go. The page had pretty much turned. Sometimes something pops up requiring a little booster shot, but for most of us the videotape is turned off and starting to gather dust.

<u>They forgive as they are forgiven</u>. When it comes down to it, anyone who forgives can hardly tell the difference between feeling forgiven and doing the forgiving.[88] We are such a mixture of sinners and sinned against, we cannot forgive people who offend us without feeling we are being set free ourselves. Jesus spoke of this eloquently.

This last point made me reflect on the fact that forgiveness often seems most difficult for those who were most vulnerable when they were victimized. Children who were born into the movement not only did not have any choice in being there but were also powerless to respond. Those who joined to escape abusive situations, only to be re-victimized in the group, also face a more challenging path to a place where they can forgive. When I first came to Jesus it was with an acute sense of my own sinful nature, so my need for forgiveness was easy for me to accept. During my life in the movement, I was also aware of some of my sinful behavior against others, incurring more "debt." After leaving the movement, I slowly became aware of another whole set of behaviors that I eventually came to realize were pushing me even more seriously into red. My actions had been contributing to the propagation of an abusive system and had caused my children (and others) to carry the scars of a confusing, erratic, and sometimes abusive upbringing. Once again I needed to seek forgiveness from both God and man. On top of all that, there is all that stuff I did today—before breakfast. I need so doggone much forgiveness that for me it really is a no-brainer. I sure as heck need to forgive, because I'm standing in such obvious need of forgiveness myself.

I know that there are so many ex-members, both first and second generations, who suffered much more abuse than I did, were in far more helpless situations, and were never in positions to contribute to the abuse themselves. That has got to make it a lot tougher to forgive. As a former leader in the movement, I may be the last one to be pointing toward this sort of advice. After all, I am one of the ones standing in need of the forgiveness of others. Nevertheless, it might help to consider the experienced voice of someone who labored among the spiritually and physically abused for years.

Dr. David Seamands is a former missionary (and missionary kid) as well as a longtime pastor whose years of experience in counseling led him to share his perceptions in several widely read books, including the classic *Healing for Damaged Emotions*. He is recognized for his careful blending of clear biblical theology, solid psychology, and practical common sense. He has worked extensively with abuse victims, many of them from within the religious world.

In his book *If Only: Moving Beyond Blame to Belief*, he presents a biblical study of the phrase "if only," examining passages where it is found in scripture. He weaves in case histories that deal with the issue of forgiveness and its role in getting past the crippling impact of serious abuse. He recounts one particularly moving story involving a college coed named Charlene, whom he had been counseling for some time. She had been the victim of many forms of abuse in an outwardly legalistic religious home. After many months of progress, Seamands finally felt the time had come to raise the issue of her willingness to relinquish the past to begin a new life:

We were seated together in my office and had started a time of prayer. I could sense Charlene's struggle with some very painful memories as we prayed for the grace for forgiveness. Suddenly she stopped, stood up, and walked over toward the wall and began sobbing as she stared out the window...she turned and said in a tone filled with bitter sadness, "I can't give them up. I'm sorry, but I just can't give up my resentments. I can't give them up. They're all I've got!"[89]

After more counseling, twice more they approached the issue without success. She abandoned counseling and melted back into the student body, never to return. Seventeen years later, Seamands was speaking in a distant state when she approached him, identified herself, and with tears spilling down her cheeks said, "Oh, Doc, two divorces and one nervous breakdown later, I guess I really should have given them up." Then she walked away. How tragic. Seamands goes on to observe, "By clinging to the pains of her past, the 'if onlys' of blame had become the keystone in the arch of her personality. She had built her life around them so that her victimization was the basis for her identity."[90] Hanging on to resentments is a way abuse victims can hang on to a sense of control. Learning to let go of them can be the most difficult area of growth for victims, as it goes against their survival instincts. Charlene's abusers clearly did not deserve her forgiveness, but it is also clear that she did not deserve the cycle of pain she ended up living with, or the tragic results.

One other aspect of forgiveness that I have struggled with is concerning the damage done to my children by others. If I have suffered personally at the hands of another and choose to forgive, that seems like my prerogative. However, can I justly extend forgiveness to those who have hurt others in my care? Somehow this seems to rub our sense of justice the wrong way. It is easy to see how this could be viewed as cavalier and uncaring, even oblivious to the way of nature. When I read about parents whose children are killed by a repeat drunk driver, or a criminal or a deranged gunman such as happened to those Amish families, and observe how they will sometimes find the path through their pain to forgiveness, it moves me deeply. The situation where the victim is alive and the pain is ongoing complicates the question, it seems to me. I think here we need to remember that forgiveness does not preclude justice where possible and appropriate. I need to remember each of us can only do our own forgiving. Sensitivity to the feelings of the offended one seems vital, and a process that supports that could possibly be helpful, but only from the sidelines. I would not want to fail to validate their feelings and choices. I greatly admire the magnanimity of my family, and their brave efforts in pursuing their own healing.

One last point that occurred to me while working on this section was about those psalms known as the "imprecatory psalms." These are the ones that are full of rage and indignation at the psalmist's enemies, where he cries out for blood. "Oh daughter of Babylon, who art to be destroyed...happy shall he be that taketh and dasheth thy little ones against the stones,"[91] and that sort of thing. It is hard to see how that sentiment lines up with the injunction to love your enemies. But perhaps these are there to acknowledge that sometimes that is how we can feel. Scripture does not endorse that position, but it does recognize the feeling as completely human. Honestly, I'm not sure if the sentiment would ever help the Edomites or Babylonians see the error of their ways, but it might help the reader say, "Yeah, I know what you mean." Acknowledge the righteous indignation. Let it out, hopefully keeping in mind that dashing anyone on the stones will not really help solve anything. It might also be helpful to keep in mind that Jesus said that those who cause a little one to stumble would be better off having a heavy millstone tied around their neck and be drowned in the midst of the sea. Whatever God has in store for these unrepentant offenders, it seems a safe bet that when He repays with vengeance it will be far more effective then anything Tony Soprano can come up with.

The Bible does not imply that forgiveness will be easy. In one scene we read, Peter comes up to the Lord and seems to be wrestling with some particularly difficult brother. He asks, "How oft shall my brother sin against me, and I forgive him? Till seven times?"[92] (perhaps feeling a bit generous). Jesus answers, "I say not unto thee until seven times, but until seventy times seven." My guess is that Peter's reaction might not have been overly enthusiastic. Jesus then proceeds to relate a story to him, leaving him with something to chew on. It is a parable in which a king compassionately forgives one of his servants a huge debt of ten thousand talents. Soon afterwards that same servant turns around and harshly enforces a relatively insignificant debt, grabbing the debtor by the throat, and despite his pleas for mercy, tosses him into prison until the debt is paid. Word of this gets back to the king, who calls for his servant and rebukes him saying, "You wicked servant! I forgave all the debt because you begged me. Should you not also have had compassion on your fellow servant, just as I have had pity on you? And his master was angry and delivered him unto the torturers until he should pay all that was due him."[93]

The point that struck me here, and I'm guessing struck Peter as well, was that it wasn't for debt that we suffer torture. The king is ready to have compassion on our debts. It is unforgiveness that leads to a torturous prison. Ultimately, as Smedes points out, it is we who have the power to open our own prison door. Or, as writer Anne Lamott puts it in her own inimitable way, "Not forgiving is like drinking rat poison and waiting for the rat to die." A helpful household hint.

CHAPTER 19

AND NOW, BACK TO OUR STORY...

We all feel the riddle of the earth without anyone to point it out. The mystery of life is the plainest part of it...every stone, or flower, is a hieroglyphic of which we have lost the key; with every step of our lives we enter into the middle of some story which we are certain to misunderstand.

~ GK Chesterton, *Orthodoxy*

*We live our lives forward,
but we understand them backwards.*

~ Soren Kierkegaard

There is a lot of discussion these days about the concept of "Story." For centuries Christendom shared one common overarching narrative, a "mythology" that imbued life with transcendent meaning, an interpretive grid through which the Western world could process its shared experience. During the last few centuries of modernity, and now into the postmodern era, this common outlook has gradually collapsed.

SOMETHING SOMEBODY STOLE

As we saw in looking at Eric Hoffer's analysis of movements in *The True Believer*, the sixties were sort of a perfect storm scenario for spawning new religious movements like hurricanes swirling out of the South Atlantic. The Family, like many other similar groups, offered us a new and captivating story we could join into, like the hobbits and dwarves and such on a quest to recover lost treasures and save worlds. For much of our time in the movement, our lives were invested with a certain "power of myth." The intensity of our shared life and unique sense of identity (skewed though it was) gave us such clear self-definition. We weren't just traveling the world, we were conquering it. We weren't just living together, we were an army on the move. We weren't just eeking out on existence, we were key players in the climactic final scene of humanity's great drama from Adam to the Heavenly City. Yeah, we could lose track of that while doing dishes or diapers or enduring rebukes, but this sense of story was continually reinforced at each morning devotions, each quiet reading time, and each evening's inspiration—as well as virtually every video viewed, song listened to, and quotation memorized or shared throughout the day.

Upon leaving the group, we found ourselves suddenly having to cope with a far less coherent picture, one that was absent of any clear mythological reinforcement. We no longer shared in the strength of a unified support group. Now we were dealing not only with the dishes and diapers, but all the loose threads unraveling from the patch of cloth that had just been torn out of the tapestry. A small sense of emotional letdown is to be expected.

When we retire from the cast of the melodramatic soap opera of cult life, relocating ourselves in a new story is unavoidable. Do we just resign ourselves to a "See Dick and Jane" world of simply surviving? Or should we track down a safer, more culturally mainstream religious environment, this time careful to make sure our set of rules and regulations can be better defended by chapter and verse? Or can we allow our souls the risk of seeking a vision that may be a little more captivating?

AND NOW, BACK TO OUR STORY...

Quite honestly, simply rejoining normal society did not quite cause my innermost being to quiver with excitement. Numerous poets, writers, and social critics have pointed out the "lives of quiet desperation" that many live, hollow men in the wasteland. The real nowhere man is still living in his nowhere land making all his nowhere plans for nobody. Any half-alert person will have noticed that one need not join a cult to be "institutionalized." The search for the perfect doctrine doesn't seem to set the heart ablaze either. Blaise Pascal carried a message he'd written on sheet of paper and then sewed into his jacket lining, next to his heart: "Fire...God of Abraham, God of Isaac, God of Jacob, not of the philosophers and scholars..." I think I can understand his determination to hold on to his vision and not let God be reduced to an add-on to a comfortable lifestyle.

So where were we to go to reorient, to rejoin the big and beautiful story—a story we hope will not only be true but will also be inviting?

Perhaps it is wise to begin with our own story. Somehow we have to try to understand our own personal biographies if we are to be in any way able to see how the tale, with all its ragged edges, might somehow be rewoven into the larger tapestry of life. In the book *To Be Told,* Christian therapist, educator, and author Dan Allender observes: "The future is meant to be written in light of patterns from the past. We can't predict the future, but we can read the patterns of the past to see how God has marked us for his purposes. He uses the past to open our future. As we learn to read the patterns, we gain understanding of our calling."[94]

Fredrick Buechner talks about this principle in *Listening to Your Life*. He writes:

If God speaks anywhere, it is into our personal lives that he speaks...through the events in all of their complexity and variety, through the harmonies and disharmonies, and counterpoints of all that happens...We cannot live our lives constantly looking back, lest we be turned into pillars of regret. But to live without listening at all is to live deaf to the fullness of the music. Sometimes we avoid listening for fear of what we may hear, sometimes for fear we may have nothing at all but the empty rattle of our own feet upon the pavement...But "be not afraid," says another, "for lo I am with you always, even unto the end of the world." He says he has been with us since each of our journeys began. Listen for him. Listen to the sweet and bitter airs of your present and your past for the sound of him.[95]

It takes time and painstaking reflection to begin to see how our messy pieces can reconnect with the masterpiece. I must confess, this is not the line of thinking that was streaming through my mind most of this time. Life sounded more like recess at an overcrowded daycare center than a symphony. Very rarely did anything resembling a string section pierce through the hectic confusion of our days. Our approach to life resembled the government's response to Hurricane Katrina: crisis management—done poorly.

Yet somehow life went on. As the kids grew older, we all gradually figured out ways to muddle through. The system was little less scary as each month the bills got paid. We stumbled into a small business—distributing a unique Christian media product—that tapped into our spiritual values and utilized some of the personal communication skills we had developed through years of street evangelism. This allowed us to begin getting a toehold on our financial future, and have a pretty good time while doing it. Our marriage calmed down, with a few smiling faces starting to sneak back into our family photos. Progress, while maybe not exactly marching on, at least scooted along. We began to believe that God was still monitoring our prayers, even if it did sometimes feel as though we were launching them up toward the end zone like Brett Favre trailing late in the fourth quarter.

Eventually we managed to work in a little time for reflection. We wondered if our lives were beginning to take any recognizable shape. Where were we supposed to fit in? Did God have any kind of blueprint in His vest pocket? We wanted to believe that, but we

AND NOW, BACK TO OUR STORY...

were sometimes haunted by the voice of cynicism. We wondered with Charlie Brown: if we were to start running toward the football to try to kick it one more time, would Lucy again pull it away at the last minute, our leg carrying us into the air to land, once again, unceremoniously on our butts? Where was it all going? Could we really allow ourselves to be open to hope that there really is a plan, a good plan, for our lives? The prophet Jeremiah wrote to encourage the disheartened and dislocated captives in Babylon, sharing with them a promise from God:

I know what I am doing. I have it all planned out—plans to take care of you, not abandon you, plans to give you the future you hoped for. When you call unto me, when you come and pray to me, I'll listen. When you come looking for me, you will find me. When you get serious about finding me and want it more than anything else, I'll make sure you won't be disappointed.[96]

I love the way Eugene Peterson, in his modern paraphrase *The Message*, not only reintroduces us to the "macro" story, but also reminds us of how our "micro" stories connect up with it. He introduces the first Gospel with these words:

Matthew opens the New Testament by setting the local story of Jesus in its historical context...(He) tells us the story in such a way that not only is everything precious to us completed in Jesus; we are completed in Jesus. Every day we wake up in the middle of something that is always going on, that has been going on for a long time: genealogy and geology, history and culture, the cosmos—God. We are neither accidental nor incidental to the story. We get orientation, briefing, background, and reassurance. Matthew provides the comprehensive context by which we see all God's creation and salvation completed in Jesus, and all parts of our lives—work, family, friends, memories, dreams—also completed in Jesus.[97]

If we can begin to get the flow of God's plan in creation refreshed in our consciousness, and through thoughtful reflection begin to recognize that same creative force working in all the "harmonies and disharmonies" of our own stories, then seeing how we can realign our paths to run in sync with the Big Story becomes easier to imagine. Meshing the sprockets and gears becomes a renewed possibility. That sense of things having come apart can begin to give way to a sense of how they can, and in fact do, come back together in the Jesus story. He came to bring not only our own internal springs and sprockets back into alignment, but also to reconnect our internal workings back up with the overall Grand Design, "wheels within wheels."

In *The Fellowship of the Ring*, during a brief pause in the action, Sam poses this question to Frodo: "What sort of a tale have we fallen into?" Sometimes it helps to get a better sense of this question by mentally employing the filmmaking technique of pulling the camera farther and farther back, exposing a wider and wider angle, helping to situate the local shot in the context of a much larger picture. The view goes from a closeup of one character to a broader landscape, to an aerial view of the town, and eventually we see the city shrink to a tiny dot on the ever-receding shot of the planet, solar system, and galaxy. It gives me a little more of an eternal perspective on things.

In their popular book *The Sacred Romance*, Brent Curtis and John Eldredge point out that if we begin the human story with Adam and Eve we haven't gone back far enough.[98] Long before that chapter God is already in eternal relationship within the Trinity. This perfect intimacy beyond our wildest imagination is actually the very heart of reality. This is the true source of our destiny. Paul describes it this way in his letter to the Ephesians:

Long before He laid down earth's foundations, He had us in mind, had settled on us as the focus of His love, to be made whole and holy by His love. Long long ago He decided to adopt us into His family through Jesus Christ. (What pleasure He took in planning this!) He wanted us to enter into the celebration of His lavish gift giving by the hand of His beloved Son...Long before we first heard of Christ and got our hopes up, He had His eye on us, had designs on us for glorious living." [99]

AND NOW, BACK TO OUR STORY...

If we can begin to reconnect these puzzle pieces, the picture itself begins to appear less random and more comprehensible; less chaotic and more anchoring. Admittedly, the picture isn't quite as neat in my mind's eye as that cultic color-by-numbers chart that we used to have in our heads. The image now seems more like a Monet, or a Van Gogh, blurry edged but full of movement, light and shadows. The colors tend to bleed into each other. But, wow, it touches something deep inside that all those neater picture puzzles don't reach. This landscape connects me in a much more profound and real way with the Artist.

The Apostle Paul was a guy who'd experienced the physical presence of the risen Christ on several occasions. He wrote much of the New Testament and was granted knowledge of things that he could not lawfully report. If anyone ought to have all his ducks in a row it would be him. Still, he had to admit, "We see through a glass darkly," or as Peterson renders this passage: "We're squinting in a fog, peering through a mist."[100] That makes me feel a little better.

In the timeless epic *Pilgrim's Progress*, at one point the hero Christian is in need of guidance on his quest for the Celestial City. Evangelist points the way and asks, "Do you see yonder wicket gate?" Christian looks off in the distance and replies, "No." Evangelist points again and asks, "Do you see yonder shining light?" Christian peers off into the darkness, and finally sees a spot that does not seem to be as dark as the rest of the darkness, and he says, "I think I do." "Keep that light in your eye," Evangelist states. "And go up directly thereto, so shall thou see the gate." Yeah, that sounds about right. When you see a place not quite as dark as the darkness around it, head that way.

Apologist Ravi Zacharias observed that "the answer to suffering is more relational than propositional."[101] In the Gospels Jesus' followers often exhibited that need for reassurance when they were challenged to take a step of faith. One stormy night on the Sea of Galilee the disciples catch a glimpse of a shadowy figure coming towards them, walking on the water. Their first reaction was, understandably, fear. Yet Peter yearns for that trusting, water-walking relationship. He calls out, "Lord, if it really is you, bid me come to you." That is a pretty big "if," which I know I can relate to! Jesus reassures him with the simple invitation, "Come." Peter steps out, eyes fixed upon the one whose voice he has come to trust. For a moment fear reasserts itself, and looking again at "the wind and the waves" he begins to sink. He cries out that most eloquent and indispensable of all prayers, "Lord, save me!" To his great comfort (and mine!) the text reports, "Immediately Jesus stretched forth his hand and caught him."[102]

Faith is always a risk. Sometimes I sink. But He always seems to catch me before I completely sink, if I can just remember to call out. To paraphrase the old axiom "Jesus came to save sinkers."

But so what? Even if we manage to get past all the negative baggage of cults and culture to open our hearts again to faith in some way, we are still left with the big question of what to do about it. Can the seed be watered? Can our spiritual lives find nourishment? Even in those moments when Jesus was not with them, the disciples had each other for encouragement. Cult experience left us with conflicting impressions—there was nothing like the shared experience of a community of fellow believers to strengthen our faith, and there was nothing like a community of believers to destroy it. So where to now?

One of the pillars of our Family belief system was the utter bankruptcy of "churchianity." We were heavily inoculated against its diseases, with regular booster shots, to insure we were immune to its dangers. The religious system was "Babylon the Great, the Mother of Harlots." We were regularly reminded to "Come out from among them and be ye separate, touch not the unclean thing."[103] Turning to church was seen as the lowest form of compromise.

When we got desperate enough for fellowship, we decided to push past the negative indoctrination and give church a chance. Our first venture in this direction was a little mission church started by a delightfully loving woman who had a tender heart for the downtrodden. The church was meeting in a semi-converted warehouse located

AND NOW, BACK TO OUR STORY...

in an area heavily populated with trailer parks. As I mentioned earlier, they were extremely welcoming, and offered us some avenues of service, which was a blessing as we went through withdrawals from our identity as "missionaries." The flock, though, was largely new believers, many from broken families, backgrounds of addiction, and theologies that were like phyllo dough in a Greek pastry—both thin and on the flakey side. Despite the atmosphere of acceptance, eventually we saw that it was not very engaging or edifying for our teenagers. We decided to do some church shopping.

We were living in Florida, where churches were more plentiful than souvenir stands. It was the odd car that was not adorned with some sort of religious message. (Our car was odd indeed—it was in such bad shape I didn't think that the Lord would want to take credit for it.) We received invitations from acquaintances, and tried quite a variety of traditions, from hard-line fundamentalist to plain vanilla Baptist to some pretty far out fringe Charismatics. We found that although we could usually find at least a few lovely people, we had to admit that sometimes reality did live up to the stereotypes. One church would have a parking lot full of luxury cars while the pastor and congregation reveled in the blessings of God-who-wants-you-to-be-rich. Across the street might feature a two-hour serving of hellfire and brimstone at the First Church of the Last Judgment. As an added challenge, trying to explain our cult adventures to folks who had never "traveled beyond the Shire" often resulted in a quick decision to play our cards much closer to our chests in the future. All of this did not exactly encourage us that we were en route to finding true community. I know some folks have had very different experiences and found a church home that was to their liking. All I can say is that we did not immediately arrive at our "Goldilocks" moment.

After a few years we moved up to New England to be near some other former members with whom we shared a very close friendship. As I described earlier, there we cobbled together a little home fellowship that worked for us for a while. Geographical and biographical changes eventually brought this chapter to a close. We would still dip our toes into the church world from time to time, but for many years we definitely fit the category "unchurched" in any religious research project. My wife and I maintained some spiritual disciplines together, and we did have other spiritually significant friendships, but we remained on the lookout for someplace we might be able to reconnect with the "Mystical Body of Christ"—in a way that wasn't purely mystical.

I came across a passage in a Wendell Berry novel I was reading at this time. The book's title character, Jayber Crow, recounts his life in a small town in rural Kentucky. As a young man he'd been dismissed from a Bible college for some theological indiscretions and ended up spending his life as a barber to a tight-knit, riverside community. He eventually becomes the part-time janitor at the local church and describes his church life this way:

Sunday mornings I go up to ring the bell and sit through the service. I don't attend for altogether religious reasons. I feel more religious, in fact, here beside this corrupt and holy stream. I am not sectarian or evangelical. I don't want to argue with anybody about religion. I wouldn't want to argue even if I thought it was arguable, or even if I thought I could win. I'm a literal reader of the Scriptures, and so I see the difficulties. And yet every Sunday morning I walk up there, over a cobble of quibbles. I am, I suppose, a difficult man. I am, maybe, the ultimate Protestant, the man at the end of the Protestant road, for as I have read the Gospels over the years, the belief has grown in me that Christ did not come to found an organized religion but came instead to found an unorganized one. He seems to have come to carry religion out of the temples into the fields and sheep pastures, onto the roadsides and the banks of rivers, into houses of sinners and publicans, into the town and the wilderness, toward the membership of all that is here. Well, you can read it and see what you think.[104]

I must admit, Jayber does make a pretty powerful point. It does seem obvious to me that the Most High dwelleth not in temples made with hands. The Spirit, like the wind, Jesus said, blows wherever it wants. I did not, by this stage, feel that our lack of religious structure blocked my access to the throne, yet there was something I still hungered for. Like Bono, I confessed that Jesus had "loosed the chains, carried the cross of my shame, you know I believe it...but I still haven't found what I'm looking for."

Reading through the New Testament, it seems clear to me that since the day of Pentecost following Jesus is something of a group activity. Ex-communalists can get the willies whenever the term "communal" comes up, but our lonely hearts beat a little faster when we started thinking about "community." Jesus does promise to be with each of us always, personally, and yet there is a unique promise of His presence "wherever two or three are gathered together" in His name. Let's face it; most of the Epistles won't make much sense if you are trying to live them on your own. As St. John of the Cross put it: "The virtuous soul that is alone...is like the burning coal that is alone. It will grow colder rather than hotter."

So what to do? Some former colleagues, burned out on all things revolutionary, settle into conservative congregations, perhaps a little rigid, but safe. It's not hard to follow the logic there. Some remain attracted to the religious fringe in the direction of apocalyptic conspiracy scenarios. Others are content to leave the issue on "simmer." We decided to go shopping again.

For a while we felt at home in a small new church plant affiliated with the Vineyard Movement. We found the pastors remarkably hospitable to us and the worship generally uplifting. Eventually, though, we grew uncomfortable for a variety of reasons. Perhaps we were just too different from the general demographic, I don't know. We then spent almost two years meeting with what was labeled an "Emergent Church." We enjoyed the open-minded, thoughtful discussions and this lovely group of people. Perhaps, though, as Dylan puts it "you can't open your mind to every conceivable point of view." It fell apart after a while. We finally decided to try "buying local," and have for several years found a home with a small mainline denominational church with a liturgical tradition. Being "claustrophobic and ex-Catholic" as George Harrison put it, I was surprised to find nourishment in this place. Maybe the liturgy resonates with our childhood spirituality. I can't say exactly why, but it has made Sunday mornings something we look forward to, and we seem to be connecting with folks there.

In her book, *Amazing Grace*, bestselling author Kathleen Norris speaks of her gradual conversion and the role that regular church life, with all its warts and flaws, played in it. "When formal worship seems less than worshipful—and it often does—if I am bored by the sheer verbiage in Presbyterian worship—and I often am—I have only to look around at other the people sitting in the pews to remind myself that we are engaged in something important, something that transcends our feeble attempts at worship, let alone my crankiness."[105] Well put. I sometimes sit in church wondering what on earth possesses me to be there. Then I look around and see folks of all backgrounds and politics making the effort to get up on a Sunday morning, not for social necessity—in New England you are a distinct minority if you attend religious services regularly—but because they find gathering with others who find worship and sharing the Lord's Table of great value. Phillip Yancey likens the church to a family Thanksgiving dinner where all the oddball relatives get invited just because of their shared DNA. Yeah, it feels kind of like that. It might not be the needlepoint saying on the cover of a Whitman's Sampler box, but it is starting to sound like a plan, as they say.

That's the news from Lake Wobegon, this week anyway.

CHAPTER 20

LONG AND WINDING ROAD

*The long and winding road that leads to your door
Will never disappear, I've seen that road before
It always leads me here, leads me to your door.
The wild and windy night that the rain washed away
Has left a pool of tears crying for the day
Why leave me standing here? Let me know the way.*

~ The Beatles, "Long and Winding Road"

*When thou passest through the waters I will be with thee;
And through the rivers, they shall not overflow thee.*

~Isaiah 43:2

When I set out hitchhiking to find the truth back in Chapter One, the album *Let It Be* had just been released. The title cut had taken on special significance for me as I traveled, with "there will be an answer..." ringing in my ears. But the cut that was actually the number one song that week was "Long and Winding Road." Perhaps I should have been paying closer attention to the message in the omens.

SOMETHING SOMEBODY STOLE

It certainly has been a long and winding road, but in the end it does feel in some ways as though I have been led back home. I am back to a place of simplicity: peace, love, and God. I love what Oliver Wendell Holmes said: "I would not give a fig for the simplicity this side of complexity, but I would give my life for the simplicity on the other side of complexity." And one's life is about what it costs, apparently. As C.S. Lewis put it, "Experience: that most brutal of teachers. But you learn, my God do you learn." I would not like to go through all that again, but I would not want to trade the lessons that I've learned along the trail either.

A large portion of my view of reality remains unmapped, but I am thankful that I am not making this journey alone. I have a great deal for which to give thanks. My wife and I have been blessed to have each other through some very difficult times. Somehow our marriage, so oddly begun, has held together and grown much deeper roots in the over forty years we've shared our lives.

As of this writing, it has now been twenty years since we left the Family with such a messy exit. At first there was a great deal of embarrassing flopping around trying to figure out how to build a new life for our family. Somehow we managed to stay on the same team, believing not only in our love for each other and for our children, but also that God's love was in some way surrounding and upholding us all. That belief has been sorely tested.

I've already talked about the struggle to simply survive in the challenging circumstances of leaving a high-control group in midlife, with a large family and no credentials. I've tried to cover some of the obstacles we needed to overcome in a marriage that sprouted in such a strange environment and survived years of sexual meanderings. I also touched on the challenges of parenting close to a dozen kids through adolescence to adulthood. By the time our "baby" turned eighteen we had been parenting minor children for over thirty-six continuous years. Phewee.

This last point, parenting, has been the most difficult area to reconcile. It is one thing to come to a place of peace in my heart regarding my own personal mess. Regardless of extenuating circumstances and the social psychology involved, most of us were of age when we met the group and were responsible for the decision to join in the first place. However, living with the damage and the difficulties that cult life has inflicted upon our kids, well, I'm sure any parent can imagine, that can be a whole lot more difficult to chew through. We've had much to celebrate along the way as the kids surpassed goals and we celebrated graduations, weddings, and grandkids. Our children are amazingly resilient and have achieved a great deal. But we've also had to live with the pain of watching several broken relationships, financial struggles, spiritual and emotional turmoil, and even the intense pain of mental illness.

In the midst of all this we faced several tragedies that forever changed all of our lives and colored our entire worldview. My wife Stephanie and I lost two of our beautiful daughters in separate accidents. This sort of thing will rock anyone's world, but coming into the fragility of our already tenuous family dynamics, it was earth shattering.

The first catastrophe happened on May 9, 1997, when our daughter Aimee, at the time a dean's list college student just shy of her nineteenth birthday, was killed in a car accident. Aimee was always an incredibly loving and lively person, both honest and kind. Aimee (meaning "beloved") who was nicknamed Habibi (also meaning "beloved" in Arabic) was truly our "beloved beloved," and she remains so forever. She cared deeply for and connected deeply with every single member of our large and diverse family. Our children's ages at the time ranged from seven years old up to twenty-five, each going through their own unique challenges. We'd been out of the group for just six years when the accident happened. The shock of her loss swept through us like a tsunami. Questions about God and His plan already permeated our entire family. This ramped up the stakes a thousand fold. The fallout continues to ripple through each of our hearts right up to the present moment.

SOMETHING SOMEBODY STOLE

At the time of the accident our third daughter, Rebecca, was just entering her teen years and struggling with issues with an intensity unusual even for our family. The sudden loss of Aimee knocked Bec for a loop that would send her reeling for the rest of her life. She started having mental crises, and spent time in several psychiatric facilities. At fifteen, she ran away and spent several months with another teenage friend, scraping for survival in a biker beach town. When we finally got her back home, her life was continually punctuated by flare-ups. She was in and out of more facilities, courtrooms, and counseling centers. When she was old enough she moved out on her own, continually struggling despite years of psychiatrists and psychologists. Turbulent relationships, financial and legal struggles, and calls from emergency rooms were the norm. For those last several years she was in a turbulent marriage that brought to her life a mixture of comfort and some stability, as well as periods of wild instability. She was a strikingly beautiful girl, whose name means "captivating" and whose namesake is introduced in scripture with the expression "The damsel was very fair to look upon." Bec was blessed with a brilliant mind, stunning musical gifts, and an artistic streak she literally wore. Despite occasional spurts of improvement, her mental illness continued to manifest itself regularly and painfully. Still, we never gave up hope for her healing. Her mother was her inseparable source of unending love and support. Stephanie was absolutely unwilling to let any of the upsetting events in Bec's life in any way lessen her tenacious commitment to be there for her at any hour of the day or night. It was after one of those "any hour" nights that our troubled and lovely Rebecca passed away through tragic accidental circumstances. She just went to sleep that chilly November night and never woke up. She had recently celebrated her twenty-third birthday. Despite her personal challenges, Bec impacted many lives during her sojourn. Over five hundred people attended her wake, which required a special police detail to redirect traffic. We heard some deeply moving stories from those who came that evening. Rebecca's suffering clearly gave her a deep compassion for others.

LONG AND WINDING ROAD

At the time of this writing it has been a few years since we've laid Bec to rest. As we enter each anniversary and holiday season, waves of grief, recent and past, continue to sweep through our family. The struggle with life's deepest questions, as I mentioned before, is not just academic, but intensely personal.

The reason I include this is to simply say that even through all of this, the wracking grief, pain, and terrible, lonely shouts of "WHY?" in the night, we have continued to lean heavily upon the Lord. It doesn't make the pain stop, nor does it answer all of our questions or lessen the challenge of dealing with the haunting list of "if onlys" that scroll through your thoughts in the wake of this sort of tragedy. Nevertheless, we can honestly report that He makes His gracious presence known to us in many ways, small and large, that continually encourage us to trust in His unfailing parental love for us and each one of our children. In the story of the death of Lazarus in the Book of John, we see that when Jesus was confronted with the deep sorrow that humanity experiences in the face of such loss, it records simply, "Jesus wept." We know that He knows.

So although this series of events may seem a little off topic, it is unthinkable that I could share in any meaningful way about our spiritual journey without including this. In adjusting to life after twenty years in the group, we've had to learn to live with many unanswered questions. We grew to accept that not every bend in the road will be fully explained. We came to find a sense of His guidance, presence, and perhaps most of all, His comfort in the wake of the soul-shattering losses of the cult experience. Cult or no cult, life will eventually serve up some huge helpings of pain to each of us. At least we had some prior experience of finding Him in the dark, or perhaps being found by Him is a better way to put it. I realize this is not the experience of all of my fellow travelers. My hope and prayer is that each will be led to a place of peace in their journey. Celtic writer John O'Donahue offers these words to frame this dynamic: "When we are ready, we will be blessed. At that moment the door to the heart becomes the gate of heaven."[106] May he be right.

SOMETHING SOMEBODY STOLE

In the Isaiah passage of this chapter's epigraph, God speaks a promise of His presence to His people in times of sorrow and testing...through life's deep waters. The prophecy continues, expressing how precious His people are to Him:

So don't be afraid; I'm with you.
I'll round up your scattered children,
Pull them in from east and west.
Send them back, every last one who bears my name,
Every man, woman, and child
Whom I created for my glory,
Yes, personally formed and made each one.[107]

We have come to believe deeply in the abiding love of God. We know that on the earth we shall have troubles. But we know that is not the end of the story. That knowledge equips us to handle the troubles here and now with His help and grace.

There is a beautiful passage in the writings of the fourteenth-century English contemplative, Julian of Norwich, which resonated deeply within us when we stumbled upon it. In a series of mystical experiences, which she recorded in her classic *Revelations of Divine Love*, Julian is prayerfully asking the Lord questions concerning sin and the suffering it has caused humankind. She receives in response an expression that is one of the most widely quoted phrases in English literature:

All shall be well,
And all shall be well,
And all manner of things shall be well.

God is working throughout history, even in each of our personal histories. And in the end "all shall be well."

Until then, life goes on. Not only do we observe ourselves going through the maturation process, but we see our kids going through it as well. I promised earlier that I would get back to the story of Sarah and our children together. Sarah has remained in the group, and currently lives in Mexico. She and the children have been continuous occupants of my thought life, and a subject of much anxiety and guilt in my heart, as well as great joy. Stephanie and I count them all as family and include them in our daily prayers for each of our family members. Sarah has been exceptionally open in allowing (and encouraging) us to do the best we can to maintain a meaningful connection. It isn't easy to bridge the huge distances, both spiritual and geographical, that separate us, but we communicate regularly and visit every few years, as we are able.

Two of the daughters that Sarah and I share eventually decided, individually and at separate times, to leave the group. We were delighted that each came to live with and/or near us for several years as young adults. They have shown an amazing magnanimity towards me despite the huge gaps in my parental input. Both girls have bonded deeply with Stephanie, and have added so much to our whole family. I recently had the immense pleasure of reconnecting with Sarah's and my second youngest son while we were visiting Mexico, where he is currently living in a Family home and pursuing his creative interests. He is extremely bright and talented, and showed great sensitivity and kindness towards me, despite my absence. The other three kids also continue in the Family as of this writing. Our eldest daughter is married and living in Europe. The other two boys are in New Zealand at the moment, Sarah's country of origin, which is also the current address of their two sisters. I deeply regret having been unable to participate more in their upbringing, but my other kids would probably tell them they should be glad I wasn't around during their teen years. My "bad cop" was not always popular with my teens. At any rate, they have all shown me great charity, and are blossoming into lovely people, no credit to me—except for maybe a few of my genes.

I should mention here that the Family is in the midst of a major revamping of its teachings and practices. The leadership seems to have come to terms with the fact that the projected scenario for the Lord's immediate return does not appear to be playing out as previously scheduled. This seems to have led them to the recognition that their high-control policies and radical separation from society has left the first generation mostly aging and broke and the subsequent generations sadly ill-equipped for life in the big city. In a dramatic reversal, for whatever reason, they are now encouraging educational and entrepreneurial pursuits, and virtual independence as far as individual decision making goes. Sadly, a great deal of damage has been done, but hopefully, at least the cycle will stop here. If only this revelation had broken through a three or four decades earlier most of this book would have been utterly unnecessary. (Although, who knows? I suspect I would have been capable of finding other book-worthy ways of screwing up my life.)

The circle of the earth keeps turning. We grow older and hopefully a little wiser. I sometimes joke with my friends, "We used to be children of the sixties, but now we are children *in* our sixties!" The prophet Ezekiel had a dramatic experience at a time when Israel was suffering in exile. God showed him a vision of a valley of dry bones, scattered in a barren desert. Ezekiel comments, "…and, lo, they were very dry…our hope is lost." The Lord asks the prophet, "Can these bones live?" Zeke replies, "Lord, Thou knowest." The Lord tells him to prophesy unto the bones, and unto the wind to blow upon the bones saying "and ye shall live!" Some mornings I, too, find myself wondering, "Can these bones live?" After a little gentle stretching, some strong coffee, and more than a little prophesying, they eventually manage to fall back in place, ready to live again. As Yogi so famously expressed it, "It ain't over till its over." Who knows? It might not be over for a while yet.

Our ambitions might need a little redefining. I like Thoreau's line: "The youth gets together his materials to build a bridge to the moon, or perchance a palace here on earth, and at length the middle-aged man concludes to build a wood-shed with them."

I was listening to Terry Gross do an interview on National Public Radio with an almost octogenarian that had been playing piano at a certain Manhattan hotel for decades. Terri asked him why he had finally retired from the gig after staying for so long. He replied: "I'm going to have my eightieth birthday in a few months. I thought it would be a good time to stop and think about what I want to do with my life." Right on, brother!

In his fascinating book *Soul Salsa*, Leonard Sweet discusses the concept of living until you die in a chapter entitled "Think Methuselah." He tells the story of a well-known celebrity of the New York art world, Howard Finster. Originally a country preacher from rural Georgia, Harold had pastored churches for forty years before beginning to paint. After preaching over 4600 sermons and taking a survey one Sunday night, he found out that folks didn't remember much of anything that he'd said, including the sermon he'd preached that morning! At age sixty-five, Finster recalls, "I said to myself: 'They're not paying much attention to me. What am I gonna do? Lord, I want to preach all over the world and reach more people.' Then God called me into sacred art, and I got to putting messages on it." His unique folk art has been featured on *The Tonight Show*, in *Rolling Stone Magazine*, and in an exhibition at the Smithsonian Institute. Cool.[108]

Sweet goes on to chronicle many other late bloomers who accomplished great things later in life. Ray Kroc, Colonel Sanders, Grandma Moses, Emily Post, and Ferdinand Zeppelin all began the work for which they became famous in their late fifties or early sixties. Portuguese novelist and Nobel laureate Jose Saramago didn't start writing until he was sixty. Cecil B. DeMille produced and directed his most famous film, *The Ten Commandments*, when he was seventy-five. Verdi wrote two of his greatest operas after turning eighty. Monet finished the most famous of his water lily paintings at age eighty-six. Surgeon Michael DeBakey was regularly performing three-hour heart operations at the age of ninety.[109] Miles to go before we sleep!

Most folks facing midlife and beyond look back over their lives with some regret over lost opportunities. Ex-cult members may have a bit more to mourn over than most. But we can't afford to waste too much time chewing old bones. The future beckons.

I really do believe that there is a way, not around our past, but through it, that can lead to a renewed trust and a deeper love. The bliss you see in the eyes and body language of young lovers is beautiful to behold. But the joy you see in an elderly couple walking arm-in-arm along the beach, a love that has weathered many of life's storms together, has a beauty that can move me to tears just thinking about it. It seems to me that our relationship with God can be much the same.

There is a song I love by the late songwriter Mark Heard, which he wrote as a young man. It means more and more to me with each passing year. It conjures forth a picture that sticks in my consciousness. Here are a few choice lines:

> *Sittin' in the dark in frayed attire*
> *He feels the chill of winter comin' in*
> *He throws another log into the fire*
> *And looks into his Bible once again*
> *He learned to love the pages as a boy*
> *And sought to keep his faith alive and strong*
> *And in the face of threats to rob his joy*
> *The years have always left him with a song*
> *The rough and shaky finger scans the lines*
> *And well he knows the old familiar words*
> *He thinks of all the times they've met his eyes*
> *It's still the goodest news he's ever heard.*[110]

As I've listened to that song through the years I think about that aged man gazing into his Bible. He brings so much with him as he approaches each word on the page. The crackling of the fire, the little aches in his joints from chopping the wood, the list of chores that didn't get done that day and will be lined up waiting for him in the morning. But as he begins to enter into the scriptures, the words speak

LONG AND WINDING ROAD

to a mind and heart now crammed with memories. Thoughts spill out in all directions, calling to mind the faces from what must seem like many lifetimes. They visit children and old friends. Playgrounds and cemeteries. Celebrations and scars. Gratitude for life's graces. The words on the page call it all forth, blending words and wonders and wounds that somehow combine to whisper some hopeful message that pulls him onward still. As Alice (of Wonderland) says: "It's a poor memory that only works backwards."

At this stage I have no idea whether I will live to meet that old man. But I do think that at least he may have once been where I now am.

Life is pretty messy business. No doubt there is still a lot of stuff in my attic and basement that eventually I'll need to get rid of. Some of it, sadly, has probably spilled out into my children's attics and basements. Hopefully they've found a few things they'll want to save and pass along to their kids, too. Like all parents, we hope they do a little better along the way than we have managed.

But as I've traveled back through these twists and turns in the river of my life, through the dreams that have been shattered, the detours into nightmares, and those dreams that Dylan says "haven't been repossessed," there, washed up along the shore, I saw it...somethin' somebody stole.

ENDNOTES

Chapter 1—"Hitchhiking Back to Eden"
1   Biff Rose, "What's Gnawing at Me" from *The Thorn in Mrs. Rose's Side*, Tetragrammaton Records, 1968.

Chapter 3—"Down the Rabbit Hole"
2   Lewis Carroll, *Alice's Adventures in Wonderland*. (New York: Signet Classics, 1960) p. 21-22.

3   Anne Lamott, *Traveling Mercies* (New York: Anchor Books: 1999) p. 103. We are in love with all things Anne.

Chapter 7—"Cracks in the Dyke"
4   M. Scott Peck, *The Road Less Traveled* (New York: Simon and Schuster: 1979) p. 45-46.

Chapter 9—"Zombies and Serpents"
5   Ronald Enroth, *Recovering from Churches that Abuse* (Grand Rapids, MI: Zondervan: 1994) p. 65.

6   Steven Hassan, *Releasing the Bonds* (Somerville, MA: Freedom of Mind Press, 2000) Chapter 2. Highly recommended reading for those interested in the cult experience. See also the Web site: www.freedomofmind.com.

7   II Cor. 10:5, Eph. 4:27.

8 David Johnson and Jeff Van Vonderen, *The Subtle Power of Spiritual Abuse* (Minneapolis, MN: Bethany House, 1991) p. 20.

9 C.S. Lewis, *The Silver Chair* (New York, Harper Trophy, 1994) p. 177-178.

Chapter 10—"O Brother, Who Art Thou?"

10 Dallas Willard, *Renovation of the Heart*, (Colorado Springs: Nav Press, 2002) p. 31.

11 Ibid, p. 33.

12 Ibid, p. 33.

13 Ibid, p. 35.

14 Ibid, p. 36.

15 Ibid, p. 37.

Chapter 11—"The Fellowship of the Wrong"

16 Enroth, p. 16–17.

17 Ibid, p. 67.

18 Matthew 13:24–30.

19 Genesis 50:20.

20 Proverbs 19:21.

21 Film, *"It's the Great Pumpkin, Charlie Brown"* (Warner Bros. Home Video) produced by Bill Melendez for CBS-TV in 1966.

ENDNOTES

22 Neil Plantinga, *Not the Way it's Supposed to Be* (Grand Rapids, MI: Eerdmans, 1998) p. 105
cited by John Ortberg, *Everybody's Normal Till You Get to Know Them*, (Grand Rapids, MI: Zondervan: 2003, p. 105.

23 Ortberg, p. 105-106.

24 M. Scott Peck, *Further Along the Road Less Traveled* (New York: Simon and Shuster: 1993) p. 105.

25 Ibid, p. 106.

26 Psalm 32—The Message.

Chapter 12—"The Heart of Darkness"

27 George Orwell, *Animal Farm*, (New York, Harcourt Brace, 1946) p. 89-90.

28 Eric Hoffer, *The True Believer,* (New York: time: 1963) p. 116.

29 Ibid, p. 12.

30 Ibid p. 118–119.

31 *Diagnostic and Statistical Manual of Mental Disorders, 4th Edition* (1994), commonly referred to as DSM-IV, of the American Psychiatric Association.

32 Sam Vaknin, Ph.D., *Malignant Self Love* (Prague and Skopje, Narcissus Publicaations, 2003) p. 398.

33 Ibid. p. 399.

34 Ibid, p. 505.

35 Ibid. p. 399.

36 Ibid. p. 507.

37 Ibid, p. 399.

38 Ibid. p. 410.

39 Ibid. p. 52.

40 Ibid. p. 202.

41 Ibid. p. 13.

42 M. Scott Peck, *The People of the Lie* (New York: Simon and Schuster: 1983) p. 37.

43 Isaiah 5:20.

44 Luke 11:31, Matthew 6:22-23.

45 Hebrews 11:15.

46 Hoffer, p. 89.

47 Lennon and McCartney, "I'm Looking Through You," Parlaphone Records, 1965.

48 Jeremiah 1:10.

Chapter 13—"Speaking of the Unspeakable"
49 Jeremiah 17:1.

ENDNOTES

Chapter 14—"Your God Is Too Weird"

50 M. Scott Peck, *Further Along the Road Less Traveled*, (New York: Simon and Schuster: 1993) p. 222.

51 Ibid, p. 223.

52 J. B. Phillips, *Your God Is Too Small*, (New York: Collier Books: 1961) p. 7.

53 Ibid. chapter titles from p. 15–55.

54 C. S. Lewis, *The Last Battle*, (New York: Harper Trophy 2000) p. 81-85.

55 From Luke 24:13-32.

56 Philip Yancey, *Soul Survivor*, (New York: Random House: 2001) p. 6-8.

57 Ezekiel 34:4–5, 18.

58 Ezekiel 34:11–12, 21–22.

Chapter 15—"How Firm a Foundation?"

59 Russell's quotation from *A Free Man's Worship*" cited by Os Guinness in *Long Journey Home* (Colorado Springs: Waterbrook Press: 2001) p. 90.

60 John 7:17.

61 Psalm 68:9 *The Message.*

62 Brennan Manning, *The Ragamuffin Gospel* (Sisters, OK: Multnomah: 1990) p. 15.

63 Ibid, p. 22-23.

64 Summary and selected dialogue from the film *Castaway* (Twentieth Century Fox) 2000. Directed by Robert Zemekis, script by William Broyles Jr.

Chapter 16—"Another Look at the Book"
65 Luke 11:52.

66 I Corinthians 13:12 *The Message*.

67 Here I am thinking about six key theological influences: N.T. Wright, Eugene Peterson, Brian McLaren, Philip Yancey, Dallas Willard, and Scott McKnight. There are lots more, of course, but they have been very helpful in giving me a fresh sense of the Bible's Story.

68 Frederich Buechner, 1980 interview in *The Door*, a magazine that was edited at the time by Mike Yaconelli. I came across it on the Internet: www.christianmystics.com/contemporary/brianrobinson/frederickbuechner.html.

69 Scot McKnight, *The Blue Parakeet* (Grand Rapids, MI: Zondervan: 2008) p. 11. (An excellent and challenging book!)

70 John 5:39–40 *The Message*.

71 Alan Reynolds, *Reading the Bible for the Love of God* (Grand Rapids, MI: Brazos Press: 2003) p. 20.

Chapter 17—"This Is Your Brain on Pain"
72 Cited in Judith Herman, *Trauma and Recovery* (New York: Basic books: 1992) p. 12. This whole discussion of PTSD and its historical uncovering is largely drawn from Herman's seminal book.

ENDNOTES

73 Norman Doidge, M.C. *The Brain That Changes Itself* (New York: Penguin Books: 2007) from back cover blurb, *New York Times Review*.

74 Bruce D. Perry, M.D., and Maia Szalavitz, *The Boy Who Was Raised as a Dog* (New York: Basic Books: 2006).

75 Andrew Newberg, M.D., and Mark Robert Waldman, *How God Changes Your Brain* (New York: Ballantine Books: 2009).

76 Agnes Sanford, *The Healing Light*. (New York: Ballantine Books: 1947/rev. 1972).

Chapter 18—"The F Word"

77 http://www.christianitytoday.com/2000/001/1.38.html p. 1.

78 Ibid. 6.

79 Ibid. 6.

80 Ibid. 6.

81 http://christianitytoday.com/ct/2002/149/55.0.html p. 1.

82 Ibid.

83 www.christianitytoday.com/2000/001/1.38.html p. 9

84 Ibid.

85 Ibid.

86 Ibid.

87 Ibid.

88 Ibid.

89 David Seamands, "If Only—Moving Beyond Blame to Belief" (Wheaton: Victor: 1995) p. 86–87.

90 Ibid.

91 Psalm 137:9.

92 Matthew 18:221–14.

93 Matthew 18:23–35.

Chapter 19—"And Now, Back to Our Story..."
94 Dan B. Allender Ph.D, *To Be Told* (Colorado Springs, CO: Waterbrook Press: 2005) p. 92.

95 Frederick Buechner, *Listening to Your Life* (New York, Harper One: 1992) p. 2–5.

96 Jeremiah 29:11 *The Message*.

97 Eugene Peterson, from the "Introduction to the Gospel of Matthew" in *The Message* (Colorado Springs: NavPress: 2002) p. 1743.

98 Brent Curtis and John Eldredge, *The Sacred Romance* (Nashville: Thomas Nelson: 1997) p. 73.

99 Ephesians 1:4–6, 11–12 *The Message*.

100 1 Corinthians 13:12 *The Message*.

101 Ravi Zacharias, *Cries of the Heart* (Nashville: Word: 1998) p. 89.

102 Matthew 14:24–33.

103 II Corinthians 6:17.

104 Wendell Berry, *Jabyber Crow* (Washington D.C.: Counterpoint: 2000) p. 320-321.

105 Kathleen Norris, *Amazing Grace* (New York: Riverhead Books: 1998) p. 268.

Chapter 20—"Long And Winding Road"

106 John O'Donohue, *Anam Cara* (New York: Harper Collins: 1997) p. 87.

107 Isaiah 43:5–7 *The Message.*

108 Leonard Sweet, *Soul Salsa* (Grand Rapids: Zondervan: 2000) p. 41-42.

109 Ibid, p. 42-43.

110 Mark Heard, "Well Worn Pages" from the album *Fingerprint* (Palm Front Communications: 1980). Available on Via Records (1995) under license from Fingerprint Records, Inc. I just went crazy when I stumbled on Mark Heard.

Made in the USA
Middletown, DE
29 September 2016